PEN‹

ANOTH‹

Alex Kerr is an American writer and Japanologist whose previous books include *Lost Japan*, *Dogs and Demons* and *Another
Kyoto* (with Kathy Arlyn Sokol). He was the first foreigner to be
awarded the Shincho Gakugei Literature Prize for the best work
of non-fiction published in Japan. Having first visited Bangkok
in the 1970s, since 1990 he lives half of each year in Kyoto, the
other half in Bangkok.

Another Bangkok

Reflections on the City

ALEX KERR

PENGUIN BOOKS

PENGUIN BOOKS

UK | USA | Canada | Ireland | Australia
India | New Zealand | South Africa

Penguin Books is part of the Penguin Random House group of companies
whose addresses can be found at global.penguinrandomhouse.com

First published in Thailand under the title *Bangkok Found*
by River Books 2009
First published in Great Britain by Penguin Books 2021
001

Copyright © Alex Kerr, 2009, 2021

The moral right of the author has been asserted

Set in 10.4/14.55 pt ITC Galliard
Typeset by Jouve (UK), Milton Keynes
Printed and bound in Great Britain by Clays Ltd, Elcograf S.p.A.

The authorized representative in the EEA is Penguin Random House
Ireland, Morrison Chambers, 32 Nassau Street, Dublin D02 YH68

A CIP catalogue record for this book is available from the British Library

ISBN: 978-0-141-98717-0

www.greenpenguin.co.uk

Contents

Foreword

T his 'meditation on Bangkok' first came out in 2009, published by River Books under the title of *Bangkok Found*. Now it's twelve years later, and I've revised it in light of Bangkok's more recent changes. In the meantime, in 2016 I wrote a book called *Another Kyoto*, which looked at the city of Kyoto based on the 'lore' accumulated from years of living there. On revisiting *Bangkok Found*, I saw that it shares a point of view with *Another Kyoto*, hence the new title. That point of view is to probe the heart of the old culture lying behind the new city.

In Japan, bookshelves sag under the weight of books in English about ceramics, *ikebana*, gardens and the ways of thinking that have inspired them. People come to Japan on bended knee, eager to soak up the Zen wisdom of tea ceremony. You don't find this in Thailand, and it's because Thailand is mostly seen from abroad as a place for fun and relaxation, shopping and the beaches. Few would imagine the existence of a rich traditional culture from which you could learn something of value.

In Bangkok, as in Japan, a vibrant popular culture abounds on every street corner. My quest has been to seek the deeper, older wellsprings of those things.

While I've written about the city of Bangkok, this also tells the tale of a journey, by a man who started out in one place and ended up in another. While American, my background for over fifty years has been Japan. A writer friend once described me long ago as: 'a youth who loves in Japanese, lives in Japanese'. Now that I'm much older, that's still true.

And then, I came to Bangkok. In a break with everything in my former life, I arrived to live permanently in this city when I was over forty years old. Thai culture had lots of surprises in store, causing me to go back and question much that I'd taken for granted in Japan, and in the end, my thoughts on Thailand congealed into this book.

Some chapters mirror those on Japan, such as the ones on old houses and performing arts, yet reach very different conclusions. Other chapters take up new subjects, such as slums, food, sex and nightlife.

I've written this for people who, like myself, have come here and have been wondering, about simple things. Why do Thai dancers' fingers bend backwards? Knowing full well that the 'Thai smile' is not always so charming, why are we still charmed?

Behind these things, enriched with input from India, Java, Cambodia, China and the West, flows one of Asia's deepest, and at same time kaleidoscopically complex, cultural traditions.

The starting point is the huge modern city that Bangkok is today. With one turn of the kaleidoscope, we see the colour and chaos that's such a familiar image of

Bangkok in the world. With another turn we see the hidden rules of order that give Thai life a sterner edge, and also its stability, peace and grace. The journey to this new city takes us back to the origins underlying it all.

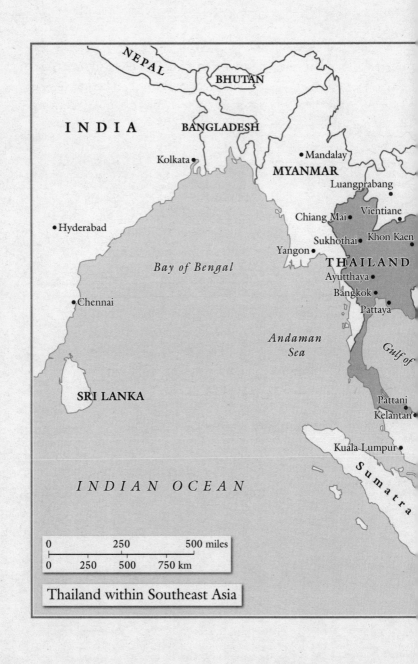

NEPAL

BHUTAN

INDIA

BANGLADESH

Kolkata •

• Mandalay

MYANMAR

Luangprabang •

Chiang Mai •   • Vientiane

• Hyderabad

Sukhothai •   Khon Kaen •

Yangon •

THAILAND

Bay of Bengal

Ayutthaya •

Bangkok •

• Pattaya

• Chennai

Andaman Sea

Gulf of

SRI LANKA

• Pattani

Kelantan •

Kuala Lumpur •

S u m a t r a

INDIAN OCEAN

| 0 | 250 | 500 miles |
| 0 | 250 | 500 | 750 km |

Thailand within Southeast Asia

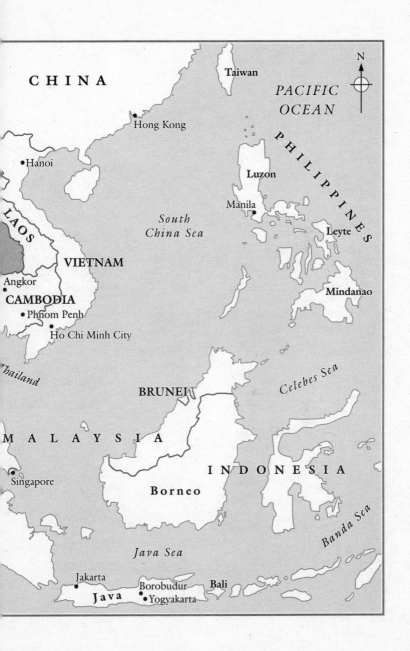

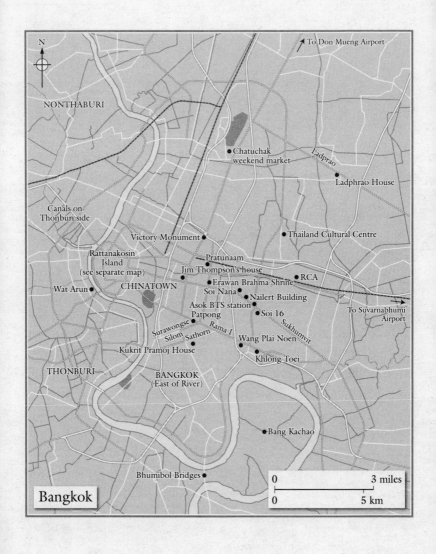

N

To Don Mueng Airport

NONTHABURI

Chatuchak
weekend market

Ladprao

Ladphrao House

Canals on
Thonburi side

Victory Monument

Thailand Cultural Centre

Rattanakosin
Island
(see separate map)

Pratunaam

Jim Thompson's house

RCA

Wat Arun

CHINATOWN

Erawan Brahma Shrine

Soi Nana

Nailert Building

Asok BTS station

Soi 16

Patpong

Sukhumvit

Surawongse

Rama 1

Wang Plai Noen

Silom

Sathorn

Kukrit Pramoj House

Khlong Toei

To Suvarnabhumi
Airport

THONBURI

BANGKOK
(East of River)

Bang Kachao

Bhumibol Bridges

0		3 miles
0		5 km

Bangkok

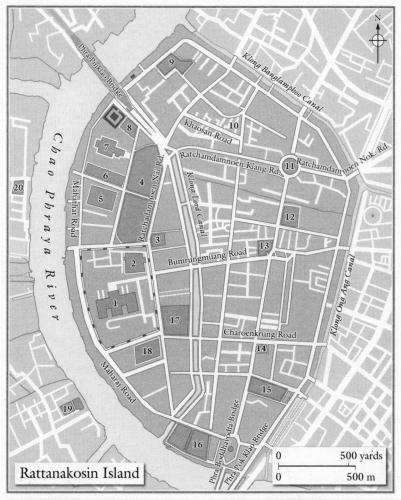

Rattanakosin Island

1 Grand Palace
2 Emerald Buddha Temple (Wat Phra Kaew)
3 City Pillar (Sao Lak Muang)
4 Royal Ground (Sanam Luang)
5 Mahachulalongkorn University/Wat Mahathat
6 Thammasat University
7 National Museum (Phutthaisawan Chapel)
8 National Theatre
9 Baan Phra Arthit
10 Khaosan Road

11 Democracy Monument
12 City Hall
13 Brahmin Temple (Devastan)
14 Sala Chalermkrung Royal Theatre
15 Pahurat Market
16 Flower Market (Pak Klong Talad)
17 Saranrom Park
18 Wat Pho
19 Temple of the Dawn (Wat Arun)
20 Patravadi Theatre (1992–2014)

The City Pillar 1
ศาลหลักหลักเมือง

เขตพระนคร

O n 28 December 1989, I was seated reading a newspaper on the bullet train going from Kyoto to Tokyo, when a voice from on high boomed in my ears and proclaimed one word: Bangkok!

In the next instant, I could hear only the hum of the speeding train. In all my life, it was my first and last visitation from heavenly spirits. Putting down my newspaper, I thought what this could this mean. The fact was that until that moment I had practically forgotten Thailand, which had accounted for a few interludes in my life in the 1970s. I had not seen Bangkok in over ten years.

My life until then was largely lived in Japan. My family came to Japan in 1964 when my father, an American naval officer, was posted to the base in Yokohama. I was then twelve years old and found a fascination with Japan that inspired me later to study Japanese and Chinese and, after 1977, to take a job and live in Japan permanently. By 1989, when the Voice spoke, I was working for the Oomoto Seminar of Japanese Arts near Kyoto, writing about Japan, doing business in Japan. There seemed to be no reason why I would ever leave.

But, as I sat there on the train, memories of Bangkok flooded in.

The First Wave

I can see that my experiences with Bangkok came in waves, each one drawing me a little closer, until at last in 1997 I washed up on shore. The first wave came when I visited Bangkok in 1975, on the way back to America after a summer in Japan. In those years before the Khao-san Road area became an international backpacker mecca, young travellers stayed at the Malaysia Hotel on Soi Ngamduplii. It was the nerve centre where you could pick up information about any place in Thailand, Nepal or beyond, from papers stuck up on the message board in the hallway.

In the city, I experienced what backpackers still do today: I wandered Chinatown, set a bird free at Wat Pho, marvelled at the Grand Palace and boated to the Floating Market. The streets brimmed with intriguing things for sale. I bought one of my first antiques on that trip: a fifteenth-century incense burner picked up at the flea market in Sanam Luang, the square in front of the palace.

While wandering around Sanam Luang, I also stumbled on the Shrine of the City Pillar, a small structure sheltering a golden column to which streams of worshippers brought flowers and incense. My companion, a Thai student guiding me around in order to practise his English, read me the history from his text book: 'Fifteen days after his coronation in 1782, King Rama I set up the city pillar here to mark the founding of Bangkok, and only later did he start constructing the Grand Palace. The exact moment of the raising of pillar, as fixed by the astronomers, was 6:45 a.m. on 21 April 1782.'

In a whisper, he added, 'We believe that when this pillar was raised, they sacrificed human beings to be buried beneath it so that they would guard and protect the city.'

The reason I made the trip was a pilgrimage to meet John Blofeld, an authority on Daoism. John had lived in Beijing in the twilight years of the 1940s before the Communist takeover, and he had inspired me with his books about exploring the secrets of the Dao with paleskinned immortals who dwelled in cloudy hermitages in China's remote mountains. John was part of the diaspora of 'old China hands' who, after the Communist victory in 1949, had relocated around Asia, some to Taiwan and Hong Kong, others to Japan. John had chosen Bangkok.

Navigating a maze of back streets, I sought out the guru. Off the traffic-choked main avenues, Bangkok was still leafy, even rural, in those days. John Blofeld lived in a traditional Thai compound. Above the dogs and screaming children in the muddy yard below, John presided serenely on the verandah of a wooden house raised up on stilts. He sat me down on the terrace in front of a golden Burmese Buddha and proceeded to expound Daoist arcana, and other secrets, such as why roofs in Thailand and China curve upwards at the eaves.

It is, he explained, to purge a taboo. When you raise up a building, you are breaking a taboo against the earth – and so the eaves, rather than pointing back down at the earth, should rise again at the tips to point up towards the sky. Since then I've heard other explanations, probably more accurate historically, but I never look at curving Thai or Chinese rooflines without remembering that conversation.

At that point, I saw Bangkok as a stop along the way, not as a destination in itself. So, just as young travellers continue to do today, I used Bangkok as a jump-off point for a trip to Burma. Returning after a week in Burma, I felt relieved to find creature comforts like air-conditioning, and also a slight sense of disappointment. Compared to Rangoon, where most people still wore *lungyi* (Burmese sarongs) and the largest structures to be seen in cities and in countryside were golden pagodas, Bangkok seemed like just another crowded dusty Asian city.

I visited Bangkok a few more times during the 1970s, usually on the way to Burma or Nepal. Then, in 1977, my long university years ended and I took a job at the Oomoto School of Traditional Japanese Arts, outside of Kyoto.

Ping and His Family

The Thai connection restarted when a young Thai from Bangkok, Ping Amranand, came to attend the Oomoto Seminar. At Oomoto, while studying Noh drama and tea ceremony, Ping and I became fast friends. In 1977, I went to Bangkok to visit Ping, and it was on this trip that I first started to think of Bangkok as a place to live.

Ping came from an exotic background, having been introduced to us as a 'Thai prince who lives in a palace'. Ping explained that he was not a prince, and only his mother, not himself, had a noble title; and the palace was a place his grandfather had purchased and which Ping sometimes visited but never much lived in. But he was in fact a descendant of King Rama IV.

Ping's family was heavily Anglicized, so much so that his aunt Nunie spoke better English than she did Thai. His mother, Pimsai, who died the year before I saw Ping in Bangkok, wrote eloquently in English, penning a book on gardens, and evocative memoirs about her childhood in England and later return to Thailand. Most of the family were educated in England, including Ping's brother Pok, who had studied at Oxford.

The British influence went way back. Ping's great-grandfather, Prince Svasti, was the first Siamese to study at Oxford. However, what fixed Britain firmly in the family's destiny was the coup of 1932 that abolished absolute monarchy. King Prajadhipok (Rama VII) went into exile in London in 1934, abdicated in 1935 and remained in England for the rest of his days. Ping's mother and her sisters grew up in London, where their father served the exiled king. Only in 1951 did they return to Bangkok.

During my week in Bangkok, Ping took me up for a weekend to the old capital of Ayutthaya, where we explored seventeenth-century ruins and paid our respects at one of the temples with his grandmother. Naked children with topknots swam in the canals, a glimpse of something soon to disappear; nowadays one only sees a

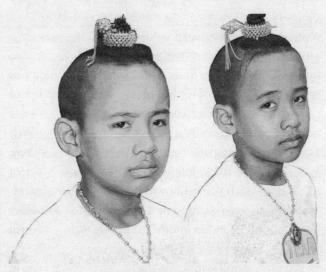

Boys with topknots: Topknots were cut at about
twelve to fourteen years old.

scene like this painted on tourist trinkets. As the grand-mother entered the temple, everyone fell to their knees.

Back in Bangkok, an interminable drive through hor-rible traffic would bring me to a quiet, leafy road off Sukhumvit, and there I'd find cheerful Nunie, Ping's aunt, surrounded by her helpers and disciples, mixing up vats of dye and melted wax for her small factory of tie-dye fashion. One of her disciples was later to visit Oomoto along with Nunie's daughter Oy and in time became one of Thailand's leading fashion designers.

But at that point we were all still young, and Nunie's atelier had more the feel of a hippy establishment than haute couture. Nunie and the gang of cousins who sur-rounded her – Ping, Ing and Oy – became an adopted family for me. Nunie had a scholarly bent and was a goldmine of information on traditional Thailand.

Looking back, I realize that the milieu I had fallen into with Ping and his family was part of the huge extended family of Thai minor royalty. Earlier reigns had enormous harems (King Rama IV had 43 consorts, Rama V had 153), producing hundreds of princes and high court ladies, who built their own palaces, a few dozen of which still stand in Bangkok today. Their descendants were honoured with titles, following the Chinese system of nobility, in which you go down one rank in each genera-tion, until finally you become a commoner. So the titles are diminishing, and in another thirty or forty years will mostly disappear.

The nobility still features on the boards of companies, in high society and in politics. In 2009, M. R. Sukhumbhand

Paribatra, scion of a noble family, won election as mayor of Bangkok. However, the land ownership that gave the nobility much of its power is dissipating as siblings break up larger plots on the death of their parents, and families sell property bit by bit to keep up their lifestyle.

It used to be said that there were three powerful groups in Bangkok: the nobility, the army and the Chinese businessmen. Of these, the nobility is fading. That leaves the army and the Sino-Thai businessmen as heirs to the city. Of course, in those days I hardly knew about this background, because Ping, Nunie and their family never talked about any of this.

I went back to the Shrine of the City Pillar and this time learned a little more. When he established the pillar, it is said that King Rama I was following a Thai tradition of erecting a wooden pole to mark the centre of each town or village. But Nunie cautioned me: 'Don't believe everything you read. City pillars, as they exist in big towns today, are not the ancient Thai things that everyone imagines. They actually derive from the stone Shiva lingams that stood in the great temples in Angkor. So they're really Khmer in origin.'

Bangkok by Night

The pleasant time spent with Nunie and her family was during daylight hours. On this visit I was more prepared to see what the night had to offer. When darkness fell, my friend Bobby Bird, son of an American-Thai family, came to pick me up in a car filled with his friends, and we would go off careening madly through the streets.

And so, by accident, I fell into the exotic nightlife of the 1970s. Bangkok was a smaller town then. When Baron Krupp flew into town and threw a big party on the boat *Oriental Queen*, handing out as party favours diamond rings and rubies to the prettiest boys and girls, all the people I met at night with Bobby were there. So was the young fashion designer whom I met during the day at Nunie's studio. At one point Bobby arranged for a Venetian bank owner to host his international guests at an old Bangkok mansion for a party – that lasted for a month. They had nineteenth-century costumes tailored for all the guests, as well as waiters, cooks and servants, who were trained in palace etiquette. A truckload of orchids arrived every day.

Bangkok at that time reflected the hedonistic abandon of the post-1960s liberation and pre-AIDS era, a decade when London and New York, too, were at their most decadent. A party for a month, entirely in antique costume, with an endless supply of fresh orchids, was one form it took in Bangkok.

Mixed-blood Bobby's high position in Bangkok's social world contrasted strongly with what I was familiar with in Japan, where people like him lived mostly on the margins. Meanwhile, Thais had been living and studying abroad for generations, as you could hear in the clipped British accents of Nunie and her children.

All this made Bangkok feel truly 'international' in a

way I'd felt before in New York, but never in any other Asian city. Bobby, and the foreign-educated Svastis, were misfits in their way, and yet they had successfully built niches for themselves in Bangkok. It made me feel that I, too, could create a life here.

Bangkok began to exert its spell. I made plans to move here and work as an English teacher. I knew next to nothing about Southeast Asia, but nevertheless, I made my decision to leave Japan. Nunie arranged for a job and even a little house in Bangkok. When I returned to Kyoto in December 1977, I was all set to announce my departure to Oomoto.

There was just one little cloud on the horizon. The night before I left Bangkok, Nunie did a divination using the old Chinese book of hexagrams called the *I Ching*. When I asked how my Bangkok life would go, we got the hexagram *The Abysmal*. 'In the abyss one falls into a pit,' the *I Ching* said. 'Misfortune.' And sure enough, on arrival at immigration in Osaka, I made the mistake of marking on my health card that I'd had a bit of diarrhoea. Armed guards rushed me off to a hospital, where they kept me in solitary quarantine for a month. A friend later said they were right to hospitalize me, but it should have been for mental reasons – for being naive enough to write the truth on the health card.

As the *I Ching* had foreseen, Japan was not ready to let me go, for immediately on emerging from the hospital, something happened that changed everything: I met the Kabuki actor Tamasaburo and became infatuated with Kabuki actors and their world. Before I knew it, all thoughts of Thailand had flown my mind. I wrote to Nunie to say I wouldn't be needing the job or the house. I spent the next few years submerged in the backstage of the Kabuki Theatre. Japan reclaimed me. A decade went by without another visit to Bangkok.

During those ten years, there were some twinges. My father, after retirement, sailed around the world for years on a small yacht, and at Christmas 1983 I went to visit him in Tahiti. One evening, I took the ferry from Tahiti to nearby Moorea, where we were anchored. It was dusk, and the Tahitians were lounging in the evening breeze, men and women wearing flowers in their hair scented with coconut oil. As they murmured soft syllables of Tahitian in gentle ripples of sound, the evening light gleamed off their smiling white teeth.

At the stern, seated squarely on a stool, legs akimbo, was one of those ubiquitous Chinese shop ladies: dressed from head to toe in black satin, with her hair pulled back in a bun and her face in an unmoving frown. The fierce Chinese madame and the gentle Tahitians, although co-existing for generations in these islands, belonged to completely different cultural universes. I thought to myself at that moment, 'I've spent most of my life in North Asia, but it's the south and the islands – they're my people!' I felt for an instant the tug to Thailand, but the moment passed, and after that I forgot again.

And yet, when the Voice from heaven spoke on the bullet train in 1989, I knew instantly what it meant. A seed planted long before had been quietly growing for the previous decade. It must be a classical pattern for midlife crisis – something inside that had been buried so deep I hardly suspected its existence burst forth, and there was no resisting it. At the time I had a busy life in Japan and had no idea what to do in Thailand, or even what the country would now be like. Nevertheless, by the time that train reached Tokyo, I had made up my mind: I was moving to Bangkok.

Arrival at Last

And so, nervous but filled with anticipation, I found myself, on 11 April 1990, driving through Bangkok's dark streets on the way to the hotel. The first thing that struck me was the darkness, such a contrast to brightly lit Japan. Bangkok has brightened considerably since then, but that night the darkness lent the city an air of invitation. Images of street carts, children selling flowers and people lounging in front of shophouses filtered through my taxi windows as I drove through those shadowed avenues. I knew this was the right place for me.

During the following week, I made another pilgrimage to the Shrine of the City Pillar. It had been rebuilt in 1986 and looked rather different from what I remembered. This time there was not one pillar, but two. One was tall and thin; the other was short and fat.

Which one was the true City Pillar? Guidebooks said nothing about it; nobody I asked seemed to know. In

Shrine of the City Pillar: (*left*) the pillar of King Rama IV;
(*right*) the pillar of King Rama I.

fact, they didn't seem even to have noticed that there
were two pillars.

I did a bit of research. It turns out that tall thin one
is the original City Pillar put up by Rama I. When first
erected, it had contained within (or below it) the horoscope for the city, which, it is said, had a lot to do with
the Burmese who had invaded and sacked Ayutthaya in
1767. However, by the time of Rama IV, it was apparent that the big threat to Thailand was not the Burmese,
but Western colonial powers.

So in 1852, not long after he acceded to the throne,
King Rama IV had a new horoscope cast and a new City
Pillar (the short fat one) put in place of the old one. Rama
I's pillar was removed and stashed against the shrine wall,

which is where it had been standing in the shadows for over a century, unseen by most visitors (including me), when I had first visited.

In the 1986 restoration of the Shrine, officials rediscovered Rama I's pillar and stood it up again so that it joined Rama IV's pillar in the duo we see today. But although they now stand side-by-side, Rama IV's shorter pillar is considered to be the true centre of Bangkok.

I learned that other old cities, such as Ayutthaya, had city pillars too. The funny thing was, though, that despite having visited Ayutthaya repeatedly in the 1970s, I just couldn't remember ever seeing the city pillar there. I went to Nunie, who laughed, and said, 'Well, of course you didn't see the one in Ayutthaya because it didn't exist. These things aren't ancient; they're quite new. Most of the city pillars we see now trace back to Phibul Songkhram (Thailand's dictator for much of the 1930s and 1940s). Officials saw city pillars as advancing Thai identity, and so they set them up in other towns, and now people think they've been there for ever. The reason you didn't see a city pillar in Ayutthaya when you went before is that they only put it up some time in the 1980s.'

So the City Pillar that represents the heart of Bangkok turns out to be two pillars, not one. As for the other city pillars, including even in the ruins of ancient Ayutthaya, far from being misty relics from ancient history, they're the inventions of modern bureaucrats.

They were installed to strengthen 'Thai identity' – but the tradition they celebrate came from Cambodia. Meanwhile, the story of human sacrifice, in which many

Bangkok dwellers still believe, also turns out to be myth, Bangkok's original 'urban legend'. No evidence exists that such a thing took place. This was my introduction to the slippery, dualistic world that is Bangkok. History is largely an illusion; and where there is one pillar, there is always another.

The questions surrounding the City Pillar made me realize that learning about Thailand was not going to be the straightforward course of study I was used to in Japan. So began a gradual process, where I would travel back and forth, spending larger amounts of time in Thailand. In 1990, I met my partner of the next sixteen years, Khajorn; in 1991, I rented my first apartment. Soon I was addicted to Bangkok and spending three or four months of each year there.

Although I was coming often, during this phase I was basically a tourist. It's a common lifestyle for foreigners who live part-time in Bangkok. Thousands shuttle back and forth between their home countries and Thailand, just as I did. Tourist life in Bangkok was exciting and *sanuk* (fun), with excursions to Pattaya and the island of Samet, restaurants and Saturday afternoon at Chatuchak Market.

Life got more exciting in February 1991, when a military coup toppled the elected government, and by spring of 1992, a civil uprising against the military junta filled Bangkok's streets. It ended in tragedy, with soldiers shooting scores of demonstrators around the Democracy Monument.

The events of 1991 and 1992 were my first coup in

Thailand, but not my last. Revolutions came and went and could even have a *sanuk* side in Bangkok, as we were later to see in the coup of 2006, when people offered flowers to the soldiers and dressed their babies in khaki to be photographed next to submachine guns and tanks.

Over the next three decades, as the anger in the demonstrations has grown more heated, and the government crackdowns more far reaching, the coups have come to feel a lot less fun. *Sanuk* was a mirage. But in the mid-1990s these more sober days were still far ahead.

Finally, in August 1997, the big moment came. I took a larger apartment that would fit my books and belongings, packed them up and shipped everything to Bangkok in a container. I sent out a letter to all my friends announcing my departure from Japan, and this time when I consulted the *I Ching*, I got *The Creative*. It said, 'Sublime success.'

On 5 September 1997, some friends gathered in the big empty apartment to which the furniture and books had not yet been delivered. We popped open a bottle of champagne and toasted Bangkok. I had finally arrived, twenty-two years after my first visit, and eight years after the Voice spoke on the bullet train.

Well, not quite. The karmic bonds with Japan hold strong. Despite having moved to Thailand, to this day I still spend about half of each year in Japan, maintain a home in Kyoto and continue writing and speaking there. Japan keeps its hold on me, and I can see now that it always will. In a sense, I've ended up like the Shrine of the City Pillar – an old life and a new life standing side by side.

While I've learned much since then, Thailand will always remain a challenge. My life has been in Japan. My heart lay in Thailand. Eventually, after many zigzags along the way, the life finally followed the heart to Bangkok.

Lightness
กระจ่างบางเบา
เขตสว่างแดนดิน

I was simply stunned when I first saw the roofs and towers of the Grand Palace across the expanse of the Sanam Luang grounds.

Decades later, no matter how many times I view it, from far away across the river, or walking by in the evening when the illuminated spires glow with orange light, I get the same thrill. The reason that I found the City Pillar in the first place was that I was hanging around the neighbourhood of the Grand Palace, fascinated by its radiant splendour. But what could be more hackneyed than this?

The Grand Palace.

Some things – *Mona Lisa*, the Taj Mahal – become so familiar from a thousand postcards and internet images that we stop looking at them and forget what makes them truly masterpieces. The same is true for Bangkok's Grand Palace, to which every tourist is dragged whether they like it or not. Glitter and whimsical carvings everywhere – it's hard to take seriously. But, as happens with cultural icons, the very thing that seems clichéd is where the wonder lies.

Few would say that Bangkok is beautiful. As fond as I am of this city, I wouldn't try to make excuses for that, because it's my belief that an attractive environment is important and that people really need it. It's East Asia's tragedy that, all the way from Japan down to Indonesia, historic towns have suffered brutally from modernization, and the new cities built in their place offer little to please the eye.

People grumble about the ugliness of Bangkok. I'm often asked how I could stand it. It's assumed that any-one with a love of beauty could never live here. And indeed, most of the city does consist of mildewed cement, corrugated tin and snarled utility wires. But they're not giving enough weight to the Grand Palace. So long as it stands, truly exhilarating beauty will always be with us in Bangkok.

For my aesthetic friends from New York or Tokyo, the palace, outrageous in its golden extravagance, offends their faith in modern minimalism. Twisting *chofa* finials, inlaid ceramics gleaming on every surface, statues in Technicolor of celestial maidens with bird tails – it's all too much. It's the Asian equivalent of Ludwig's fairytale castle in Bavaria.

Which is to say, charming, but trivial. Open a book dedicated to the great monuments of Asia, and you will see illustrations of Angkor Wat in Cambodia, the Forbidden City in Beijing and Kyoto's Gold Pavilion. You would almost never see Bangkok's Grand Palace. It falls under the category of 'tourist curiosity', not under 'art' or 'architecture'. The Sanam Luang grounds in front of it also would not show up as an example of a great 'city square'. Yet the view from Sanam Luang rivals Red Square and Tiananmen for dramatic effect, and outdoes them both in magic.

The Grand Palace
As heritage sites go, the Grand Palace is rather young, built mostly in the nineteenth century. It lacks the cosmic

structure of Beijing's Forbidden City, with its central axis and grand courtyards. Instead, it's a higgledy-piggledy collection of structures of every shape, built at the whim of successive kings. In line with the vague, anti-historical essence of Bangkok, the Grand Palace grew not according to a human plan, but naturally, like a forest.

Before Bangkok, Ayutthaya had been the capital of the Siamese Empire since the fourteenth century and in its heyday was one of the larger cities of the world, rich with golden palaces and pagodas. Its sack by the Burmese in 1767 came as a massive blow to the national psyche. After some decades of turmoil, when a new line of kings re-established the Siamese empire in Bangkok, they styled their metropolis as a copy of the vanished glorious capital. The city and the palace were one giant sigh of nostalgia for a mythical past.

Ayutthaya itself harkened back to the Khmer Empire at Angkor, with input from Laos, China and as far afield as Persia. So when the kings of Bangkok started building, they drew on a vast vocabulary of cultural forms.

The tall cigar-shaped *prang* towers (Mount Meru, symbolic centre of the world, topped by Indra's trident) evolved from the towers of Angkor. The twisting *chofa* finials that rise from eaves and roof beams came down with animist Thai tribes when they descended the river valleys from China.

Chofa finials are deeply old, coming to us from a time when people believed in naga serpents and gods of the land and sky. It seems likely that the rising eaves of Southeast Asia went north and became the typical curved roofs of China. At some point, Chinese rooflines began to curve, and it appears this originated in the animist south.

The farther north you are, the straighter the roofs, as you can see in the Forbidden City, with its stern and formal structure. When you travel south below the Yangtze, roofs become more and more fanciful, and in the far south they twist upwards like candy curlicues, encrusted with so much stuff that you can hardly see where the roof starts and ends.

The power of these roofs has intrigued me ever since I was a student visiting Bangkok for the first time in 1975 and made the pilgrimage to meet John Blofeld. Maybe John's 'Taboo Theory' was correct – it was because these roofs look away from the earth and turn to the sky – that they were later able to sweep all before them in China, Korea and Japan. At a deep level they satisfy a craving in the human mind. Hence mankind's love of minarets, obelisks and skyscrapers. The genius of upward-turned eaves is that it transforms every rooftop into skypointing fingers.

Ayutthaya in its heyday, with its royal temples, *chofa* finials and *prang* towers, was the model of a divine city. After its destruction, the memory of glorious Ayutthaya lived on as a gleaming ideal of Siamese greatness. So the new royal city of Bangkok copied the old as closely as possible: they dug a canal to the east of the river to duplicate Ayutthaya's oval-shaped island; they built the Grand Palace, and within it a royal temple, and next to it a 'Front Palace'. They named temples to remind them of

Rising eaves of East Asian architecture (clockwise from top):
Forbidden City in Beijing (north China); bell tower in Nara (Japan);
Thai temple; temple in Hangzhou (south China).

Ayutthaya, such as Wat Mahathat, the Temple of the
Holy Relic. Surrounding the royal temple stand *bai sema*,
leaf-shaped monoliths which demarcated sacred boundaries in ancient times. This shape also is echoed in the
crenellations of the palace's surrounding wall.

What got built in Bangkok contains a wealth of cultural

reference that would be hard to find in almost any other structure in the world: wall paintings of India's Rama-yana epic; peaked windows from Persia; rooflines from the Thai tribes' old homelands in the north; towers and Hindu gods from Angkor, 'demon mask' motifs from Java; stone guardians and bonsai from China; stupas from Sri Lanka: trapezoidal doors from Ayutthaya. Plus thrones modelled like boats, and demons and angels from all over the place. The Grand Palace is a gigantic treasure box, filled with the accumulated lore of East Asia.

It happened just in time. By the end of the nineteenth century, when King Rama V was putting the finishing touches on the Grand Palace, the pressure of Western-led modernization had made it already an anachronism. The palace complex in Bangkok is the last great archi-tectural undertaking to rise when Asia's old ideals were still intact.

Ethereal Architecture

Most people would, of course, hardly be aware of all this. What strikes visitors seeing the palace for the first time is simply the effect of dazzling fantasy. The basic structures came mostly from Sri Lanka or Angkor, but almost every form has been stretched out. While built of heavy stone, the twinkling complex feels insubstantial.

That lightness is a calculated effect, crafted in royal

Buddhist sculpture: curved eyelids, eyebrows and fingers.

Ayutthaya. It's part of a long process, whereby over the centuries buildings stretched taller, windows narrowed, stupas got sleeker, columns tilted inwards, and every surface came to shine with gold and reflective inlay.

The Thais have been doing this to imported culture for a long time. They took the squat bell-like stupas of Sri Lanka and stretched them out to produce the bud-shaped soaring *chedi*. In the Sukhothai Period, they took the sombre-seated Buddha in meditation and lifted him up so that he was walking (descending from heaven). His soft, androgynous figure treads so lightly he appears to float. The Buddha's eyebrows arched, eyelids extended, the fingers grew long and sinuous.

In the Ayutthaya Period the Thais took the chunky 'artichoke' towers of Khmer temples and lengthened them into the slim 'corncob' *prang* that surmount Thai

Khmer 'artichokes' stretched into Thai 'corncobs': (*above*) Angkor Wat in Siam Reap, Cambodia; (*below*) Wat Arun (Temple of the Dawn) in Bangkok.

temples and palaces. Over time the slimming process continued as temple walls grew higher, the multi-tiered roofs steeper.

Meanwhile, inside the dark interiors with their tall slatted windows, Ayutthaya artists craved light. They crowned statues with tiaras and draped them with jewellery; they covered walls and columns with glass mosaics and frescoes. By the time Bangkok was founded, gilding and garnish swallowed up every flat surface.

As everything stretched and tapered, the right angle disappeared.

No country in the world avoids a ninety-degree angle as Thailand does. In ancient times Thai houses were built with a natural lean to them, the walls tilting slightly inwards or outwards, to create stability. What started in wood transferred to stone, brick and plaster, and from this point onwards Thai temples departed from the stolid strength of Indian or Chinese buildings. Every angle was askew.

In Ayutthaya they bowed the bases of temples inward, to create a so-called 'elephant's belly' which looks like the concave deck of a ship: high at the bow and stern, low amidships. From these curving boat-like bases, walls rose at an inward tilt. Doors, window frames, thrones and book chests followed suit. The tilting affected things at smaller and smaller scales, to the point that even pillows and jewellery boxes all took the shape of a trapezoid.

In this land of no-right-angles, Euclidean geometry is banished; two parallel lines will always meet. Everything is slightly thinner at the top end, and the effect, a trick of perspective, is to make things look elegant and light-weight. Thai objects and buildings took on an 'ethereal' quality, delicate objects that angels had dropped from heaven.

The purpose of the palace is to express wealth, power and empire. Yet, the Thai way to do this is to commute it into lightness. The effect emanates from hundreds of

'Elephant's belly': temple bases in Ayutthaya slope
downwards like the sides of a boat.

Trapezoidal window: door and window frames taper inwards.

pillars slanting at less-than-ninety-degree angles, spires rising up to impossible thinness and flickering *Lai Thai* designs flaring upwards like bird flight or flames.

The Emerald City

The multiplicity of towers and spires and the sparkling mosaics covering walls and columns were not, as most visitors would imagine, just a way of making things prettier. Behind them lies a philosophy, encapsulated in the fourteenth-century Traiphum (Three Worlds) cosmology. The Traiphum describes a hierarchy of worlds, rising from hell, to our earth, heaven and beyond to nirvana. Our world centres on a cluster of sacred mountains encircling the highest mountain of them all, axis of the universe, supreme Mount Meru.

Mount Meru is a pan-Asian theme that stretches from India (where it originated) through China and up to Japan. As codified in the Traiphum cosmology, Meru is the centre of the universe, at the peak of which sits Lord Indra with his trident.

Thai temples and palaces were built to symbolize the ranges of sacred mountains, each one taller than the last, which rise shining and gemlike from our world into heaven. Those mountains are the many spires of the palace.

In the Traiphum it's written that Mount Meru, when seen from our continent, looks bright and crystalline,

radiating emerald light. Hence the twinkling surfaces –
they're the emerald glow of magical Mount Meru.

Emerald-green is the colour of Indra, who is lord of
the Hindu gods and at the same time a guide of Buddha. It's also the colour of Rama, Vishnu's avatar, who
was associated with Thai kingship from Ayutthaya times.

With both Indra and Rama taking the colour green,
acquiring the Emerald Buddha from Vientiane in Laos
was an essential first step in the founding of Bangkok.
The official name of Bangkok – the longest city name in
the world, with 168 letters – contains the word *Rattanakosin*, 'Gem of Indra', which is emerald, of course,
and Rattanakosin is still the name used for the old central city. Right from the start, the colour of Bangkok was
green. They had the green city, so they brought the
green Buddha here.

The Temple of the Emerald Buddha, which stands at
the heart of the Grand Palace, is where we get closest to
Indra's emerald beams radiating over the royal capital.
The rest of the palace is one huge sparkling frame for
this emerald jewel. The sloping pillars and glittering
ornaments tell us that we're no longer on earth; we're at
the cosmic centre, gem-like abode of the gods.

The lightness of the palace is not accidental; it's the
world's most extreme statement of lightness. Lightness
isn't everything, of course. There's nothing to compare
with the restful harmony of an old Zen garden in Kyoto.
Just as the Thais make serious things look light, the Japanese make modest, day-to-day things look momentous.
A tea bowl, lumpy and brown, has all the gravity of a

weighty mountain. The moss gardens of Kyoto anchor us in the earth. In contrast, the palaces of Bangkok lift us up to heaven. When away from Japan, I miss the mossy calm of old Kyoto. But when away from Bangkok, I long for the shimmering towers that carry me skywards.

For Thais, the Grand Palace resonates at another level, stirring something deep in their hearts, because it conjures up the world of old kings, queens and their courts, with all the ritual that swirled around their lives in those scintillating throne halls and inside the taboo courtyards of the royal concubines.

In China, a century after the last emperor ceded his throne, Tiananmen, the gate to the Forbidden City,

Royal Crematorium of King Rama IX:
Phra Merumas spires at Sanam Luang royal grounds, October 2017

still acts as an irresistible magnet for Chinese national consciousness. The Forbidden City's palaces are so far removed from the realities of life in present-day China as to practically come from another planet, yet new generations still stand before them in awe. In Thailand, where kings still reign, the palace is not just a historical relic – even the most jaded youth of Siam Square carry the imprint of the Grand Palace's towers and gables somewhere deep in their souls.

This was brought home after the death of King Rama IX in 2016, which was followed by massive funeral observances held at Sanam Luang, the royal grounds facing the palace. After lying in state, the king's body was brought to a specially built Royal Crematorium (Phra Merumas), itself a miniature palace and, as the name *Merumas* indicates, a literal Mount Meru. Surrounding it, like the seas and mountains of Mount Meru, were lesser towers and pavilions, ponds and the mythical animals of Himmaphan, the sacred forest at the foot of Mount Meru. After the cremation in October 2017, the grounds were opened for several months to the public, who wandered through its splendours of decorative art.

In May 2019, the palace and its surroundings were again the scene of lavish ceremonies as King Rama X was enthroned inside the palace and afterwards paraded with his entourage through the streets around the royal grounds. Both the cremation and enthronement were presented on live television, revealing every glamorous detail to the public.

We've learned as Westerners to guard against the

The Grand Palace: in summer, kites fly over Sanam Luang, the Royal Ground in front of the Palace.

tendency to see Asia through the eyes of the 'exotic'. Exotic is something that tourists seek; it's not an acceptable emotion for a serious student of the culture, much less a long-term resident.

But in Bangkok, you simply have no choice but to give into the exotic sparkle. Especially when the palace roofs are lit up at night with the moon rising behind. Or in March, when hundreds of people are flying kites in Sanam Luang, and you glimpse the spires of the palace across the grounds with snaky tails of kites fluttering about.

The Grand Palace of Bangkok is an exotic fantasy, hardly a thing of this world. Its makers intended it to be exactly that.

Land
ที่ดิน
3

เขตปลอดโฉนด

I t was early 1991, and Khun Sukrit was trying to sell me an island. Displayed on the walls of his spacious Bangkok office, large colour-coded maps showed the pieces of the island that he had succeeded in buying, and the patches that remained in the hands of local fisherman. Located just a short boat ride from Phuket, this island was ripe for development into a prime resort and villa destination.

Khun Sukrit hailed from Phuket, where he had made a fortune, much of which he had poured into acquiring his island. To the side of his desk stood a Buddhist altar, flanked by an array of oval *phanphum* about 20 cm tall in the shape of lotus buds. Originally flower offerings made of folded banana leaves, they now come in durable plastic as well as aluminium for home and office use. Sukrit's were made of gold and silver.

Only recently, Adrian Zecha, legendary developer of the Aman Resorts, had opened his gorgeous Amanpuri on Phuket, which set the standard, not only for vacationing for the super-wealthy, but for the business of selling villas. The villas adjoining Amanpuri, it was rumoured, retailed for a million dollars apiece. This earned Zecha a luxury hotel for free plus a war chest of extra cash. Khun Sukrit had found an even better property, overlooking a more picturesque beach, and he owned most of the island, so the resort and villas could be absolutely exclusive.

Phanphum:
altar decorations in the shape of lotus buds.

In the glory days of the 1980s, when Japan's economic boom was at its height and the Japanese were buying up the world, I was working in Tokyo, representing Trammell Crow, an American real estate developer based in Dallas. By 1990 Japan's bubble had burst. However, I knew that Bangkok was in the middle of its own boom, and so I convinced the Dallas headquarters to pay for me to search for projects that we could introduce to our investors in Japan.

At first I relied on local Thai friends, who drove me around outlying areas of the city and showed me great patches of empty land that were mostly reedy swamps. I learned the Thai measurements of land: *tarang wah* (4 square metres) and *rai* (1,600 square metres).

A foreigner or a foreign corporation cannot legally buy or own land in Thailand. In those days, foreigners could not even own an apartment. However, you could invest in a Thai firm, or lend money to a real-estate venture. Possibilities were everywhere: much of Sathorn was still lined with decaying mansions. Drive deep into the *sois* (side streets off the main avenues) and you would come across empty plots only a few metres from a housing estate. Richer Thai friends were purchasing land as fast as they could. One of them would get in his car on a Sunday morning, load the trunk with a suitcase of cash and drive around the suburbs buying up fields as he went.

From Water to Land

There were reasons for those empty fields at the end of the *sois*. It had to do with the way the city has grown – with water, not with land. Bangkok was originally a swamp crisscrossed with canals, so watery that the first Western traders lived in riverboats moored along the banks of the Chao Phraya. Wide avenues like Sukhumvit and Sathorn – in fact most of Bangkok's important arteries – began life as canals, not roads. Then, as Bangkok began to expand, the city drained the swamps and paved the canals.

The loss of the old water-cities is a notable chapter in the story of modern Asia. Once towns like this thrived everywhere, as we can see from the fact that Calcutta (Kolkata), Bangkok and Edo (old Tokyo) all were once described as 'Venice of the East'. As these cities modernized, town planners treated waterways as empty space over which to build elevated expressways and bridges, and when buildings went up alongside the canals, they turned their backs to them, providing not a terrace or a door, hardly even a window to the waterway just outside.

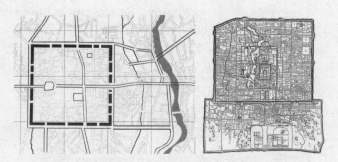

Chinese-style square cities: (*left*) Old Chiang Mai; (*right*) Old Beijing.

The change from water to land was meaningful for Bangkok because every town of central Thailand was once a water-city. Boats, not carts or horses, are how Thais got around in the old days, and the image of the handsome lad poling his boat down a lily-pad-lined river while his beloved sits behind him combing her long hair is a stock cliché of period films.

The ancient Chinese pattern for a capital city is a square, aligned along north-south-east-west axes. Most of the old capitals of East Asia followed this format. Beijing, Kyoto, Hue, Mandalay, Angkor Thom and Chiang Mai, all took the shape of the cosmic square.

In contrast, the cities of central Thailand form loose ovals, because these towns were built on islands in the rivers. Inside the loop of the surrounding river, canals sliced the city into a grid, as we can see in seventeeth-century Dutch paintings of Ayutthaya. If you look closely at a map of Bangkok, you can still make out the outline of the original oval of the royal centre, defined

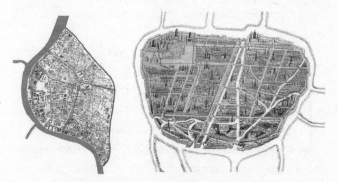

Thai-style oval cities: (*left*) Old Bangkok; (*right*) Ayutthaya.

by the Chao Phraya River to the west and the Khlong Lord Canal to the east.

While it has been nearly a century since the average Thai citizen owned a boat, the King still maintains his carved and gilded royal barges, a tradition going back to Ayutthaya days. Every few years the barges make a grand ceremonial procession down the Chao Phraya, in which hundreds of oarsmen dressed in brilliant costumes row in time with the rhythm of drums and stately chants.

The royal barge procession is not something you can witness every day in Bangkok. But there is an extensive network of canals on Thonburi, on the west side of the river, where one can still get a glimpse in a more modest way of what Thai canal life once was. Take a long-tailed boat, and within minutes of turning off the Chao Phraya onto Bangkok Noi Canal, you see houses on stilts built over water, hung with potted plants. As you go further you'll catch a glimpse of an old grandmother washing in the river, or a troupe of shrieking boys diving off a verandah for their afternoon swim. Here and there a few old teak houses still remain, teetering at odd angles.

My favourite part of the canals has always been the stretch just north of Bangkok in Nonthaburi. Few tourists get this far, since by the time they reach the more quiet rural areas, their forty-five minutes of canal tour is over. Past this point, the scenery turns green, sugar palms sway along the banks, and teak houses with pointed eaves and sculpted windows appear.

All that is far away, almost another world when seen

from the modern downtown. Bangkok went from tree-lined canals to concrete shophouse city after the Second World War. The city has spent the last fifty years expanding into marshes and farmland. One of the beautiful Thai houses of Bangkok, which belonged to former Prime Minister Kukrit, survives off Soi Suan Phlu near what is now the central business district of Sathorn. It stood among lychee groves until the 1960s. The Prakanong district of Sukhumvit was *khlongs* (canals) and rice paddies right into the 1970s.

Flat Noodles

Bangkok's spread followed a pattern: first, the early kings marked off the central 'island' of Rattanakosin, where they raised Bangkok's major temples and palaces. In the bordering areas, they pushed through the first avenues, which they lined with government offices and palaces of royal progeny. A few of these estates are still lived in by aristocratic families, but in recent decades most have been torn down or have been taken over by businesses. The palaces have disappeared into Bangkok's mishmash of shophouses and office tower blocks.

A big avenue like Sukhumvit or Ladphrao would be cut through open farmland, sometimes filling in a canal, other times bordering the canal. Soon it would be lined by shophouses. The canal would disappear. Then small *sois* would extend like tentacles growing from the sides of these avenues, and along these, people filled in marshy land and built homes. However, behind it all the swamp remained.

As you fly into Suvarnabhumi Airport you can see in the countryside outside of Bangkok long narrow plots of land called *sen kuay tiew*, named after a type of flat rice-noodle. As *sen kuay tiew* plots like these were absorbed into the city, roads grew along the edges of the 'flat noodles', so there were few crossover streets. The zigzags we see in town today formed where the *sois* had to detour around plantations and rice paddies. This pattern of growth along 'noodle strip farms' accounts for why it can be so maddeningly difficult in Bangkok to get from one *soi* to another.

I remember looking out of the window of the Dusit Thani Hotel when I began visiting Bangkok in 1990, and just off crowded Silom Road I was amazed to see what looked like acres of palm trees and banyans. In the heart of the city, the jungle was still there. Even today, you can sometimes turn off Sukhumvit or Ladphrao and suddenly find yourself among trees and large walled compounds.

On a map of Bangkok you'll see a huge green area cradled within a loop of the Chao Phraya River east of Taksin Bridge. Called Bang Kachao, it's as large in area as the entire central business district. Filled with fruit plantations, swamp and jungle, it's a protected area with hardly any roads, very few houses, no hotels and just a handful of local restaurants. Actually Bang Kachao belongs to the neighbouring province of Samut Prakarn, not to the City

Satellite view of Bangkok:
the dark 'lung' is the greenery of Bang Kachao.

of Bangkok, and only appears to be within the city limits because of the wide meander of the river. It's a matter of time before politicians manage to get beyond the restrictions, but for the time being this great swathe of green remains.

Bang Kachao is sometimes called the 'Lung of Bangkok', and it's a reminder of what all of Bangkok's environs once were. However, the true lung of Bangkok was the jungle within.

This is now changing. Builders began with plots on the main roads, such as the palaces in the old town, and the Chinese mansions in colonial style that still lined Sathorn Road in 1990 – within ten years all but one or two disappeared, to be replaced by office towers. The next step was to erect apartment blocks along side streets.

Now the developers have reached the long-empty plots behind the *sois*. The tree-filled back lanes that you used to be able to see from the higher windows of the Dusit Thani are vanishing.

For me the most intriguing project of 1991 involved an old palace on Phra Arthit Road. A big block of colonial architecture, with high ceilings and a grand wooden staircase, the house rose upwards to a picturesque 'widow's walk' turret. Built in 1932 around the time when the coup abolished absolute monarchy, this building had been the home of a princely family. From the 1960s to the late 1980s, it functioned as the Goethe Institute's headquarters in Bangkok until Goethe moved to its present grounds off Sathorn Road. The house had been empty for a few years and was falling into disrepair.

I thought it would make a great project for our Japanese investors, as a restaurant or boutique hotel, in a street that, while near the Grand Palace and Khaosan Road, was at that time still undiscovered. However, the asking price was too high for any normal business venture. Phra Arthit Palace needed to be owned by someone who wanted it just as a showpiece. Years later, just that person came along, Sondhi Limthongkul, entrepreneur owner of Manager Magazine, who restored it and incorporated it into Manager's head office.

In 2006 and 2008, the house played a role in modern Thai history, when Sondhi turned against Prime Minister Thaksin and used the Manager offices as headquarters for the opposition movement he helped launch. While I suppose this was the preordained destiny of the palace, every time I pass in front of it I remember the day I first entered its dusty rooms carrying a flashlight, and I have a little twinge of regret for what might have been.

Looking back on it, the early 1990s were the last time when one could easily find palaces for sale in Bangkok. Of course, Trammell Crow and our Japanese investors were not looking for historical romance; they wanted good returns. We looked further afield, and met up with Khun Sukrit, and his island near Phuket. Unlike the Phra Arthit Palace, which could not be redeveloped, Khun Sukrit's land provided wide-open spaces to landscape as we saw fit. It seemed ideal.

Land in Grey, Blue, Green and Pink

Until that fateful afternoon in Khun Sukrit's office. There had been a few references before then to the type of deeds that went with the island properties. 'It's all fine, nothing to worry about,' Khun Sukrit assured me. I pressed for more details and learned that in Thailand you don't just own land or not own land. There are several grades in between.

Firmest of all is *Chanode* (Full Land Title), but below this are a number of deeds referred to by their initials in the Thai alphabet. These are expressed (in English pronunciation) by adding an *or* sound to the end of each letter, plus a number. I found out that there are *nor sor 3* (certificate of land occupation), *nor sor 3 kor* (the same as *nor sor 3*, but with more definite land boundaries), *sor por kor* (registered deed of ownership, but untransferable) and three types of squatter's right: *sor kor 1*, *por bor tor 6* and *por bor tor 5*.

The colour-coded map on Khun Sukrit's wall reflected these differences, shaded in grey, blue, green, and pink. About half of the plots were coloured pink, which, I found out, stood for 'Don't know.' One could see that almost every aspect of developing this island was semilegal, or quite possibly illegal. These grey and pink areas haven't stopped other real-estate developers in Thailand. In fact, many of the resorts in the Phuket area started out in just this same way, not to mention plenty of office towers and condos in Bangkok. But for the bean counters in Dallas and the blue-suited bankers in Japan, this was going to be a hard sell.

Meanwhile, Khun Sukrit had fallen into financial difficulties. Desperate to save himself, he was asking far more than his land, a patchwork of dubious ownership deeds, was worth. Talks began to unravel. Khun Sukrit looked more and more unhappy. One day he changed offices, and the gold and silver *phanphum* disappeared.

On 23 February 1991, I and the boss from Dallas were seated at the Royal Bangkok Sports Club meeting with a developer who was pointing out that Thailand had 'political stability far beyond its neighbours'. Suddenly the television came on, and it was announced that there had been a coup and the army was taking over. So much for political stability. The boss returned to Dallas and ordered me back to Tokyo.

From that time on, I made regular trips to Bangkok on my own, living in a small rental apartment off of Sathorn Road. As I watched, Bangkok went right on booming. In 1994, an architect friend from Tokyo introduced me to one of the more glamorous figures I've known in Bangkok, M. L. Tridhosyuth Devakul. 'Tri', as he's usually known, is an architect and a real-estate developer. Some blame his Boathouse Inn in Phuket for unleashing the real-estate frenzy on that island.

And maybe it did. But as I travelled around to Tri's properties, I came to appreciate the advanced side of development in Thailand. Schooled in America, Tri brought a modern sense of design to the use of classical Thai motifs: curving roofs, open-air *sala* (four-posted pavilions) and teak pillars. By the late 1990s, Tri

High-rises with Thai-style hats: a trio of towers along the Chao Phraya River designed by M. L. Tridhosyuth Devakul.

was riding high, with a hotel completed in Chiang Rai along the Golden Triangle and a trio of residential towers along the Chao Phraya River in Bangkok, conspicuous even now for their peaked Thai roofs on the penthouses.

Then came the Great Crash of 1997. It started in Thailand and soon swept over the rest of Asia. It was the final hiccup of the bursting Japanese bubble. When the crash came to Thailand it hit much harder than it had hit Japan because Japan squandered its own money in the bubble, but Thailand lost funds borrowed from abroad. The baht lost half its value, and Thai developers' debts doubled overnight. Major banks went under, great fortunes disappeared in smoke. Tri told me at the time that he had lost 90 per cent of his net worth.

By 1997, I had moved into my present apartment at Sukhumvit Soi 16, near the Asoke-Sukhumvit intersection. Three skyscrapers were rising at my corner, and overnight the work stopped, as did hundreds of projects across Bangkok. Because Thailand had no proper bankruptcy law, banks could not repossess these properties, nor could they be auctioned off, because big business families had too much to lose. Bangkok became for a decade a city of rusting hulks. From my living room on the fourteenth floor, for eight years I enjoyed the sight of the sun setting through the open I-beams of the 'ghost buildings' across the street.

Only in 2005 did the economy pick up again. Developers came in, finished off the deserted superstructures and delivered them as condos and office blocks. Tri bounced back, as real-estate developers often do; Bangkok entered another boom.

Booms and Busts

In 2009, as the world reeled in response to the US's mortgage loan crisis, the bubble burst again. However, this downturn looked more like a 'business cycle' than the truly disastrous collapse of 1997. Thailand is more of a mature economy today. It can absorb more office and condo space, and the money isn't all borrowed from Japan. Or so we hope. With the Covid-19 crisis of 2020–21 and the collapse of tourism, once again a bust threatens.

On my side, as the booms and busts came and went, my real-estate ventures in Thailand amounted in the end to exactly nothing. To this day, I haven't invested in a single *tarang wah* of Thai property.

But many others have invested. Thailand has always been the most foreigner-friendly country in Asia, and it has long been producing a lucrative 'export product': real estate sold or rented to foreigners. In 1998, the government lifted a ban on non-Thas owning condos, and it has lured thousands of people to the country on 'retirement visas', which make it easy for older foreigners to live here so long as they bring in cash for their expenses each year.

International money pours into Bangkok and Pattaya, fuelling a market in homes and vacation rentals for Americans, Europeans and Japanese. Wealthy Russians and

Chinese are just behind them in the rush to find living space in this ever-hospitable city. Rents in Bangkok have been historically low, compared to almost any other world city, or even regional capitals such as Hanoi or Phnom Penh, which have far lower standards of living than Thailand.

It's fine to talk about culture and *sanuk* (fun), but the fact is that the cheapness of Bangkok is key to its appeal for expats. Tens of thousands of foreigners already live here, with thousands more arriving hard on their heels. Many don't reside full-time but keep a condo in Bangkok for occasional visits. As foreigners, we can live here at a level far beyond what we could achieve with similar means in our home countries. Affordability has made Bangkok international.

Low real-estate values arise from the fact that Bangkok was until recently a low-density city covering a huge area, consisting largely of *khlongs* and farmland. Also, Bangkok's openness to the outside world impacts the quality of housing available to foreigners. Spacious apartments in Tokyo are rare and 'special', with the result that the few luxury residences designed for foreigners command huge premiums. A similar dynamic is at work in Phnom Penh or Beijing. Foreigners posted to these cities by big multinationals or NGOs are all chasing after a small number of attractive homes.

Thailand has been building for foreigners for generations, and the process has nurtured local designers such as Tri, with his sophisticated mix of modern and Thai traditional. Bangkok revels in a stock of well-designed apartment buildings the likes of which Tokyo or Shang-hai can only dream of.

Like everything else, this is changing, of course, and there is no doubt that Bangkok will converge with world norms. We who've taken Bangkok's cheapness for granted are finding ourselves priced out of the market.

Back in 1995, my twenty-eight-storey building stood proudly as one of the tallest structures in the neighbour-hood, but we're shrinking as taller buildings go up around us. In 2009 the four huge Millennium Towers went up on neighbouring Soi 18. At fifty-three storeys each, they dwarf our now modest-looking condominium.

My landlord, Khun Num, grumbles, 'They look like *pret*.' And indeed they bear an uncanny resemblance to *phii pret*, a type of hungry ghost, with a tall, skeletal body, topped by a tiny head with a little needle mouth.

The Millennium Towers: four giants loom over
older buildings around Sukhumvit Soi 16.

Pret are insatiably hungry and specialize in sucking up the *bun* (karmic merit) of all they come across. Num warns that the four giant towers, topped by heliports, will start out as merely hungry for tenants. But their hunger will never be satiated until they suck all the *bun* out of Soi 16 and its surroundings.

The *bun* that's being sucked away is the street-life-oriented, chaotic, tree-filled 'village Bangkok' that once existed, in favour of high-rises and malls. In Thai ghost movies, the hero or the local abbot finds a way in the end to stop the *pret* and return them to the under-world where they belong. In real life, of course, the *pret* always win.

Shop
ร้านค้า

4

เขตเงินเงินเงิน

When planning my move to Bangkok in 1997, I went to Dallas to see my former boss, real-estate developer Trammell Crow. A swashbuckling frontiersman of the old school, he was addicted to making 'deals', to the extent that, when I worked for him, his staff had to watch him at all times, or he would agree to develop a hotel with someone he met in the elevator.

Seated in front of Trammell's desk at the top of his skyscraper in Dallas, I laid out my plans for Bangkok. There was a silence. Trammell sighed, reached into his desk drawer and pulled out ten thousand dollars in cash.

'Here's my investment,' he drawled. And added, 'You know – if this was poker, I wouldn't bet on it!'

With Trammell's funds behind me, a group of Japanese friends agreed to pitch in, and by the spring of 1997 I was ready to move to Bangkok. I prepared to transfer the investment money to Bangkok and have it changed into baht. But before that could happen the company registration needed to be completed, as well as a work visa – and we ran into the most baffling difficulties. The problem was with the lawyers.

The first lawyer got us into trouble by filing a ghost address for the company; then failed to submit papers in time; and finally had a heart attack, at which point his office lost all the papers. The second lawyer couldn't translate from English into Thai, so those papers too ended up being worthless.

By now it was late summer. The business climate in Bangkok was white-hot; we were losing our chance. This time we contacted a mainline firm and they got to work to register us as fast as it could be done. But about a week before the money was due to be wired, the Great Crash had come.

For several decades the baht had held steady against the dollar at about 25 baht to the dollar. On 2 July 1997, it began falling, and by January 13 of the next year, it had reached 55.8 baht to the dollar. Currencies collapsed all over Southeast Asia, as stock markets swooned and real-estate values evaporated. The fall in Indonesia was so severe that the rupiah shrank at one point to less than a tenth of its previous value. Within eight months,

Suharto's regime, which had lasted for over thirty years, collapsed. Thailand escaped with not much political upheaval, but the economic repercussions changed the face of the city.

By the time we got incorporated in late 1997 and I wired the money to Bangkok, the Crash had come, and the yen was now worth twice as much in baht. The smartest financial move I ever made was due to the incompetence of my lawyers.

The question now was what the new company would do. The original plan, as proposed to Trammell and the others, was to set up a programme of traditional arts such as I had managed in Kyoto. However, it became clear that I didn't know enough. I had no friends in the arts, and I wasn't even sure what the arts of Thailand would be. At this point, my partner Khajorn stepped in and urged me to open a shop selling *benjarong*.

Benjarong

Benjarong (meaning literally 'five colours') is a form of traditional Thai ceramic. Inspired in the nineteenth century by the bright colours of Chinese ceramics, Thais came up with their own patterns, with which they covered the surface of bowls and *phan* stem-cups, using enamels in bright blue, green and red, outlined in gold. The fine detail and gorgeous effect made it much prized by Thai elites, and to this day you'll often see pieces of *benjarong* in wealthy homes or hotels.

Khajorn worked in a shop in an upscale mall run by our friend Ying, a businesswoman who was making a fortune selling *benjarong*. Ying adapted *benjarong* to Western tastes, applying the patterns not only to old-style Thai shapes, but also to thin and translucent Western-style 'bone china' suitable for dinner plates and coffee cups. Foreigners snapped it up at high prices, sometimes ordering sets of hundreds of pieces.

Before I knew what happened, my company became a *benjarong* shop. Khajorn and I sat down with Ying, and she agreed to become Khajorn's supplier. We went looking for a location and found a dream spot: a glass-fronted store right on Sukhumvit Road, at the Nai Lert Building

Benjarong lidded jar: detailed patterns in bright colours embellished with gold cover the surface.

near the corner of Soi 5. It stood in the heart of Sukhum-vit's tourist foot traffic, midway between major hotels and Soi 3, where the Arabs congregate.

Rents at the Nai Lert Building were among the high-est in the city. Taking the biggest financial risk of my life, I plunked down thousands of dollars in advance rent. More thousands went into fitting out the shop with overhead spotlights, and chrome frames laid with glass shelving. Intense spotlights bathed the ceramics with light, which, reflecting off chrome and glass, brought out the golden lustre of the surface decoration and dazzled tourists into buying.

Benjarong does not come cheap, even at wholesale prices. First, we had to lay in boxes of white 'bone china' (which serves as the base) – plates and bowls in many sizes and styles. These were then sent to the fac-tories, where artisans painted them with gold and enamels. The process took months. Finally, the shop's glass shelves were lined with gleaming plates, teapots and lampstands, and in June of 1998, we opened for business.

We soon ran into trouble with Ying. Ying had the virtues and vices of a classic Chinese businessperson. She worked hard, bought low and sold high. Starting as a shop-girl, she ended up as shop-owner and at her peak drove a Rolls-Royce. Ying was also addicted to gambling and used to play with the highfliers at their illicit casino on a rooftop overlooking the river. Soon she owed millions of baht to some very unsavoury characters and ended up living life on the run to escape her creditors. Ying could no longer be seen in her own shop, had to change its name, and hide her home address. She moved around town behind tinted car windows at night. We needed to find another supply route or we too would be caught up in Ying's underworld drama.

Khajorn found his own factories. Sometimes we'd drive out to visit them in Samut Sakhon, about two hours drive from town. A typical 'factory' consisted of a tin shed on the side of a muddy *khlong*, with six or seven workers – basically a family – mum and dad, the grandmother and the children, sitting on the floor painting *benjarong*. It's a painstaking process, involving hours of work, as each thread-like gold line and each green, yellow and purple enamel dot has to be applied by hand. After painting, they dry the enamels, then fire them in an electric kiln in the front yard.

The Shop

Working with the factories was a full-time job for Khajorn. The father of one household would get a mistress, his wife would storm out, and they would cease production for a while until things settled down. At another place, we knew that they would do no work for a week after payday, since the owner would go on a drinking binge and only come back after he'd used up the money. Some factories are better at doing butterflies, some at flowers. Family A will paint in the flowers, and then family B will do the butterflies. If the butterfly people stop working, then an entire line of production might be held up for months.

Another problem was pattern stealing. Bangkok thrives on counterfeit brands and cheap copies. There's no telling how many Versaces, Versacci and Versache shops you can find around the city. Friends of mine in the export business will not show their goods in Bangkok's big trade fairs – because everything new will immediately be mimicked.

People were always trying to spy on us and steal our patterns, which they would duplicate on lower-quality whiteware and sell at half the price. Rival shops would send people over to our factories to buy a few pieces as samples.

Then there's the matter of tax reporting. At first I did my best to follow and understand it, but found that in Thailand filing is done monthly rather than yearly, as I was accustomed to in Japan. The staff spent at least half of their time just preparing documents.

So complicated did the finances become that we needed to hire an office manager. This is how Khun Saa came into my life. Saa, who happened to live across the hall from me, is a typical Bangkok story. She came to Bangkok from Prachinburi province at the age of thirteen in order to attend high school and lived with her older sister in a little wooden house on the Thonburi side of the Chao Phraya River. The sister sold *som tam* (green papaya salad) and grilled chicken to put Saa through school. Eventually Saa entered Ramkhamhaeng University, Thailand's huge open college.

Saa found a job with my neighbour, Khun Num, who ran a television production company. Under his tutelage, she learned English, computer proficiency, and, most importantly, the art of Thai bureaucracy. Listening to Saa dealing with officials and bankers, I felt the difference between Thailand and Japan.

In Japan, formality rules all. Thailand, too, requires formality, but you also need to amuse. Humour is the Joker that trumps even the Ace of propriety. While saying all the proper things, one must also draw a smile, combine politeness with the spirit of fun, that is, *sanuk*. Saa is a master of this.

Around the time the *benjarong* company was starting up, Num retired from television producing, and Saa, finding herself at loose ends, came to work for us, acting as our ever-smiling interface with officialdom.

Finding sales staff for the shop was easy – hire family. Khajorn brought in relatives from his village in northern Thailand, once part of the old kingdom of Lanna based in Chiang Mai. *Benjarong* is expensive merchandise, and at times there would be large sums of money lying around. Khajorn simply wouldn't trust anyone outside his village. The staff spoke Northern dialect among themselves, making us a little corner of Lanna in the city.

The kinship paradigm comes from China, for it's the Chinese who run and own most of the successful businesses in Thailand. The Chinese business mode has placed its stamp on companies in Thailand. Contracts and part-nerships have a limited shelf life, and you can never turn your back on any venture – employees will jump to another company without warning, taking clients and secrets with them. Best to rely on family.

This is something of a generalization, of course, and perhaps I was sensitive, coming from Japan, which falls at the other extreme. In Japan, company loyalty held an iron grip on employees' souls, having taken the place of samurai fealty to the feudal lord. People are scrupu-lously honest, at least within their organizations.

Well, all this is changing. Bangkok is going towards more predictability and professionalism. As the city modernizes and becomes more wealthy, the middle class is expanding, and business is converging on interna-tional norms.

Khajorn was an exception among shop-owners along Sukhumvit Road in that he was ethnically Thai – most of the others were Chinese or Indian. But his business style was totally Chinese, and it had to be, because busi-ness in Thailand, especially for small enterprises, still basically follows the old Chinese mode. Which brings us to the character of the city itself. My Thai friends com-plain that Bangkok is becoming a Chinese city. They see the old politenesses and easy-going give-and-take of the Thais disappearing before the mercantile rush of the Chinese.

Actually, Bangkok was a Chinese city right from the beginning. Aside from a Thai military garrison, the small town from which Bangkok developed consisted of a community of Chinese merchants. King Rama I displaced it south in order to build his capital at Rattanakosin (the old city centre), and Chinatown dates from this time. Into the new royal centre came the Thai court and its entourages, and later, the Westerners, Indians, and so forth. The Chinese are the original inhabitants of the city.

The Street

Khajorn's friends were mostly hawkers on the stretch of pavement in front of the shop. If there's one trait that until recently distinguished Bangkok from every other Asian city, it has been the street vendors. You could go out at any hour of the day or night and buy almost anything: fruit, noodles, flowers, suitcases. On Silom, as people poured out of the discos at 2 a.m., they might stop to buy a jasmine garland, some fried grasshoppers – or a pet rabbit. Part of what first appealed to me as the taxi drove into town from Don Muang Airport in 1990 was the vendors along the streets, and they have contributed much to making Bangkok a pleasurable place to live.

At lunchtime, my staff go out to a nearby market, a gathering of vendors on an empty lot, and bring back all sorts of things to eat, wrapped in plastic bags: curries, mango salad and fruits, not to mention more odorous items such as *plaa raa* (fermented fish). There is surely no place on earth where you can always find such a range of delicious and healthy foods on the street. They also bring back T-shirts, iced coffee (also in a plastic bag), and mobile phone accessories.

In Singapore, the government has seen hawkers as undisciplined, and restricted them to 'hawker centres' to the point that most of the city now consists of malls and office blocks, off-limits to vendors. In Jakarta, there never seemed to be so many vendors in the first place. It might have something to do with the Thais' natural entrepreneurism. Thais mostly aren't happy working for someone else. They'd much rather run their own business, even if small.

My experience is that Thais are dreamers. They love the lottery; young Thai friends of mine live in the hope that their little business will make them rich. In Bangkok, the Chinese merchant mind met up with Thai dreaming – and the result was an explosion into a million stands and stalls. At the low end of the scale are the street vendors, and a step above them are the booths that crowd giant markets such as Chatuchak or Mahboonkrong, each selling something unique and quirky. It's a recipe for cooking up the zany and unexpected, which is why Bangkok, above all cities that I know in East Asia, could be called truly 'colourful.'

Those days are ending. Policy-makers in modern Bangkok – some Sino-Thai businessmen, others bureaucrats, but all of an authoritarian mode – hanker after squeaky-clean Singapore. The idea is that the vendors are

Fruit vendor at Soi 16.

messy and unmodern. In the late 2010s, the Bangkok
city government has put into effect a sweeping clean-up
of street vendors, removing them first from one avenue
and then another.

The effect is transforming the city. Still, Thais are
used to buying from the street. They know where good
food is to be found – tastier and cheaper than any restaurant. This is where the mass of the city has always
found its food, drinks, clothes and flowers. A strong
need will keep the vendors alive until they are finally all
swept away. This was brought home forcefully during
the student demonstrations of 2020. In order to battle
the police, the students would appear in a flash mob at an
unpredictable time and place and then, after thirty minutes of an hour, disappear as fast as they gathered. But

they still needed food and drink. The police scrambled to keep up, but the vendors had been tipped off and were always there on the ready.

Before the anti-vendor campaigns started, the north side of Sukhumvit Road from Nana to Soi 19 used to be one of the most crowded vendor districts in Bangkok. Most of what was on sale were the usual tourist trinkets: fake watches, T-shirts, wooden phalluses. My nephew Edan, when he lived with me for a summer when he was twelve years old, made friends with a watch vendor and subcontracted the business: when a group of Australian teenagers would come along, charming Edan was lying in wait for them with ten watches on each arm. He got a commission for each sale.

The landlord controlled the pavement in front of the Nai Lert Building, so the hawkers had to stay away during the day. At night, however, they encroached, with people spreading mats lined with bracelets that light up and rows of pink high-heeled shoes. Living together cheek by jowl, the vendors in our neighbourhood got to know each other very well, and the street was rife with petty jealousies and arguments.

Khun Daeng, who sold watches at the corner, became a friend of Khajorn's and was often to be seen drinking tea inside the shop. He knew who was in trouble because of gambling debts, whose wife had run away to Khonkaen and so forth. Daeng was the man we could call on as a 'fixer' if we suddenly needed a carpenter, or a camera to be repaired. He could also introduce a bank manager or an insurance sales lady. For Edan's birthday party, we realized in the afternoon that we hadn't planned anything fun for the night; a word to Khun Daeng and he brought a troupe of magicians over to my apartment, complete with acrobats and fire-eaters.

Despite their gossip and competition, at a time of crisis all the vendors would band together. Woe betide the Dubai man who refused to pay the lady in the next block for a pair of rubber flipflops. The CD seller at the neighbouring booth stepped in, the Dubai man raised his fists – at the end of the mayhem, he was lying bruised on the pavement, and then the police arrived. Per the testimony of the onlookers, they carted the Dubai man away to the police station as the 'troublemaker', much to the delight of Daeng and Khajorn. Order had been restored to the street.

The Nai Lert Building area borders Sukhumvit Soi 3 (Soi Nana) and Soi 3½, the haunt of Bangkok's Arab population. Turn into Soi 3½ and suddenly the signs are in Arabic and you can hear Egyptian music and spot rows of hookahs in front of the restaurants.

Bangkok boasts a number of enclaves like this soi, among the most prominent of which are Pahurat (the Indian textile market bordering Chinatown), Sukhumvit Sois 35-55 (favoured by the Japanese) and Pratunam (popular with Africans). Bangkok has had extensive Asian populations since the nineteenth century.

Aside from Thais of Chinese extraction (who make up as much as 60 per cent of Bangkok's population), there are smaller groups of Arabs and Africans. Indians, many of them Namdhari Sikhs, members of a particular cult of Sikhism, dominate the tailor business in Bangkok. Indians own huge swathes of land along Sukhumvit Road, plus a number of hotels. They make up one of Thailand's richest communities, and they are often to be found in swanky clubs and restaurants. Many have married Thai wives, but the rules of Sikhism mean that while they may have lived here for generations, they're less integrated than the Chinese.

Decline and Fall

One of Bangkok's traits is that it has been so welcoming to outsiders, and this is why I was able to establish a business here in the first place. You constantly meet foreigners who have created their own business, and who run shops or restaurants. Some have succeeded fabulously.

Sadly, I was not one of them. Actually, I think it's the rule rather than the exception that foreigners put more money into Thailand than they take out. In my case, it began promisingly. We made lamps for the Oriental and Le Meridien hotels. One day a fleet of black Mercedes-Benzes pulled up in front of the shop, and military officers in white uniform marched into the shop. Khajorn thought, 'Oh my God, they've come to arrest me!' It turned out to be a delegation from the palace. A lady-in-waiting followed the white uniforms, and she ordered a set of lamps. This was the high point of the shop.

However, no matter how much we sold, it all went to pay the rent, and at the end of the month, after paying salaries and taxes, there would be little left.

As time went by, the shop lost momentum. After six years at the Nai Lert Building, we found another location on Silom, only a quarter of the size, but at far lower rent. We got a fast-food restaurant to take over the Nai Lert lease and moved to Silom.

For about two years, Khajorn sold *benjarong* at this second shop, between Patpong Soi 2 and Silom Soi 4. Vendor politics here were even more colourful than at Sukhumvit, to the point of being scary. The sock lady got into an argument with the towel lady and cut her with a knife – but the local mafia protected her, and the police never said a word. At Silom, Khajorn kept a little more distance from the street vendors.

Eventually, weary of the daily struggle with the factories and clients, Khajorn began to lose his heart for the business. Although the Nai Lert shop had never made any money, it also hadn't lost any. At Silom, however, there was a slow but steady flow of red ink. In 2004 we finally gave up. The pressures put a strain on my relationship with Khajorn, and we split up after many years.

In the end, after nearly eight years in business, I managed to lose the entire investment from 1997 and had to go back to my shareholders and admit to them that all the money was gone.

Like so many other foreigners, I came to Thailand and lost everything. Trammell's instincts had been right when he foresaw that Bangkok for me would be a bad bet. But, like my Thai friends, I continue to dream. In 2005, Saa and I started all over again, founding another company. This one, called Origin Asia, is centred on Thai traditional arts – which is what I originally thought I would do when I made the move in 1997.

Running a *benjarong* shop was a detour, one of those things one never thought one would do in life. I never drive by the Nai Lert Building at Soi 5 without a twinge of nostalgia. I remember our gleaming glass and chrome store front, and think: 'This was our shop!' I came to Bangkok intending to do one thing, and got distracted and did another. Bangkok's a distracting place.

House
เรือนไทย
5

เขตวังทองหลาง

Every year thousands of people visit Jim Thompson's house on the *khlong* and go away dreaming of how nice it would be to live in an old teak home. I was one of them. I first made the pilgrimage as a twenty-three-year old in 1975, and it came as a revelation.

Jim Thompson, the man who revived the Thai silk industry in the 1950s, put together several old teak structures to create a mansion centred around an open-sided living room framed by tall slanting columns. Bedroom, dining room and annexes, filled with antiques, radiate from this central platform. Famous from the day it was built, it became even more so after Jim Thompson's mysterious disappearance on a trip to Malaysia in 1967. When I first visited, you were free to roam the house as you wished. I spent hours there, lounging on the open deck of the living room, or seated in the study, gazing enthralled at the age-worn Mon statue, still my favourite art work in Thailand.

I had been smitten with the love of old houses since I was a little boy in Japan, when my mother used to take me to the homes of her friends. It was in the days before they tore down Tokyo's wooden homes and replaced them with apartment blocks. As a college student, with visions of those houses still in my mind, in the summer of 1973 I had purchased Chiiori, a thatched farmhouse perched high on a misty peak in the centre of the island of Shikoku.

At Chiiori, deep in the mountains, one could live the dream in Japan. Suddenly, with Jim Thompson, I saw that one could live the dream in Thailand as well, and from that day forward, I sought to find an old house in Bangkok. The problem is, of course, that the Jim Thompson dream has become nearly impossible in the megalopolis that is Bangkok. Most of the canals on the eastern side of the river, the body of the modern city, were filled in decades ago.

You have to go far out of the city centre on to the *khlongs* of Nonthaburi to the northwest to find Thai houses of any number. Here, alongside older buildings, the rich have built some grand Thai-style villas. The older cottages look charming, but rot and termites have infested them to the point that, sagging on their tall supports, it's only a matter of time before they crumble into the water. You'd have to buy land to build over the mud, and what legal title to the mud consists of is a murky prospect. In order to live up here, you'd need also to buy a boat and hire a full-time boatman. Locating along the northern *khlongs* is the equivalent of moving to the countryside: it only makes sense to live beside Nonthaburi's canals if you're ready to retire from Bangkok itself.

So I turned my attention to the city centre. Traditional Thai houses do still exist in town, such as the home of M. R. Kukrit Pramoj in the Suan Phlu area, which has been opened to the public. Kukrit was a noted writer and former prime minister. His house, with its stage for masked dance performances, and raised pavilions, faces a wide grassy garden.

Another of my favourite Thai complexes is Wang Plainoen, a teak palace near Khlong Toei, belonging to the descendants of Prince Naris, the 'artist prince' in the early twentieth century who designed Wat Benjamabopit (the Marble Temple), and acted as patron of Thai dance and music.

Wang Plainoen is filled with precious antiques, including what may be Thailand's best Khon (classical dance) mask collection. Its finest feature is the open room with a raised seating platform where Naris once held court, overlooking a garden where students of traditional dance perform in the open air – something you can go and see when the palace is opened to the public on Prince Naris's birthday in April each year.

I knew that you didn't have to be prime minister or be descended from a prince in order to live this way. The memory of John Blofeld in 1975, and his teak study raised on stilts, stayed in my mind. John lived the life of a modest scholar, the house rising from a yard full of children and chickens. Going to see him felt like spending time at an up-country farmhouse.

Of the Thai houses in the city centre, one of the most remarkable belongs to Rolf von Bueren and his family, owners of the design firm Lotus Arts de Vivre. It's located just a few minutes' walk from the busy Asoke-Sukhumvit intersection. A nighttime visit there has a feeling of magic, almost a conjurer's trick. You turn off the busy *soi* into a

Dinner pavilion in the evening: house of Rolf von Bueren.

passageway that takes you past ferns and vine-covered trees to enter the main house, decorated with Thai art, traditional and modern. The high point comes later in the evening, when your host invites you outside, and you walk across a wooden walkway built over a pond to a raised Thai pavilion, where dinner is served. Modern Bangkok is only feet away – but one has slipped into an air bubble of a time far away and long ago.

The von Buerens' little paradise would be hard to duplicate today. Traditional houses are doomed in modern Bangkok, as they are in most large Asian cities. Lack of protection for historic homes, and a feeling that these old places are old-fashioned and even an embarrassment, leave them naked and exposed to the harsh realities of urban real estate.

Looking for the Dream

In the writing of Proust, his characters live for years pining after a longed-for ideal – gaining the heart of a lover, seeing a famous actress perform – and one day a magic moment comes: they step over a threshold, and actually experience it. One haunting line of Proust captured well my yearnings for old Thailand: 'Like one who believes that he will be able to taste in reality all the pleasure of the dream.'

Still seeking the dream, I shifted my focus outside Bangkok. The obvious place to build a teak house was my then-partner Khajorn's village in northern Thailand. I saw teak houses all over Thailand being torn down and discarded and I thought I could collect some of this wood and build a house myself.

We explored towns and valleys all over the North and eventually purchased the wood of three houses, which we dismantled and moved by truck to the village. Once the wood had arrived, carpenters set about raising twenty teak columns on which the house would stand, planed flooring out of redwood, and crafted walls, roofing, kitchen and bath. On New Year's Eve 1998, my friends and I converged to celebrate the completion of the house, a symphony in golden teak pillars and redwood panelling, overlooking a lotus pond.

And there, sadly, the story stops. Like many before me who've built their vacation place up-country, I ended up almost never visiting it. The village was just too far away. I can count just a few times since then when I stayed in this lovely house. Khajorn himself, after his father passed away, moved from the village to a shophouse along the main highway, and finally he dismantled the building and used the wood for a new home in town. It all came to naught. I gave up on the idea of finding a Thai-style house and settled into a condo on the fourteenth floor of an apartment building off Sukhumvit.

Students of the occult learn that the First Law of Magic is: 'It only happens after you've given up on it.' That's why when the rainmakers come and do their dance, it always stays bone dry while they're still dancing. Eventually the onlookers tire and slip away in disappointment, and the rainmakers are sent home in disgrace, at which point it begins to pour.

True to the First Law, it was shortly after I'd moved into the condo that the miracle happened. My cousin Thomas Kerr, an architect also living in Bangkok, works for an NGO involved with slum housing, and in order to live near his office he rented an apartment near Ladphrao Soi 60. One day he was walking to work when he noticed a long wall pierced with three high-eaved gates. Above the walls could be glimpsed the peaked roofs of old houses, surrounded by flowering branches that spilled out over the wall. Tom was intrigued and knocked on the door of the first gate.

Inside turned out to be a spacious compound covering nearly a full city block. The owner, Khun Santi, was an essayist, song lyricist and food expert – a renaissance man of traditional culture – who had erected a series of Thai-style houses and pavilions. Some were old structures that he had found in his base of Ayutthaya, dismantled and brought to Bangkok; others he had built new. Santi thought that his wife and daughters would drape themselves in sarongs and lounge elegantly on the verandahs like mythical Thai ladies of old. But of course, what they wanted to do was to learn piano and travel to Paris. The family lived in an air-conditioned concrete edifice in one corner of the property, while the wooden pavilions mouldered away, and Santi worried about what to do with them.

Tom and Santi hit it off immediately. In the summer of 1998 Tom offered to move in and look after the houses,

Peaked roofs of Santi's house.

and Santi agreed to lease a wing of the property for a very reasonable rent. For him, it was a chance to see his darling houses properly cared for at last. There was more here than Tom could handle on his own, and, knowing my love for old houses, he called me in to join him.

The Secret Garden

Thus, thanks to the luck of Tom's walking down Ladphrao Soi 60, we ended up as tenants of Khun Santi's secret garden. Our part of the complex had its own gate, and when I entered that gate I always felt as if I had stepped through a hidden door into an alternate universe. You started out at hot and smoggy Ladphrao Road, with its multiple lanes of unmoving traffic. You turned on to Soi 60, zigzagged a few times until you reached our quiet *soi*, and soon you found yourself standing in front of a Thai-style gate.

You pushed open a low door cut into the gate, ducking as you entered, and when that door closed, modern Bangkok had disappeared. Ahead was a mossy brick courtyard, shadowed deeply with flowering trees and one tall fan palm outlined against the sky. To the right was a double-winged wooden house on stilts (two houses joined by an open wooden deck), which took the classic form of old central Thai homes. A flight of wooden steps, flanked by potted palms, led up to the deck. It was painted the same dark red that one sees at Jim Thompson's – originally made from crushed mineral pigment, it protects against sun and insects.

At the far end of the courtyard stood a Chinese-style chalet with a green-tiled roof, which is where Tom lived. Nearby, another flight of wooden steps climbed upwards to the *sala*, or open-sided dance pavilion, shaded by a towering banyan tree with down-hanging roots. Even though you were still very much in the city, you could hear birds twittering by day and frogs croaking at night.

The fact that the two main houses and the dance *sala* stood high on stilts is a reminder of these houses' watery origins. The stilts were to raise them above river floods or the dampness of the forest floor. But as composed by Rolf von Bueren or Khun Santi, embellished with passageways and fanciful sculptures, these houses took on an otherworldly air. The compound was Santi's dreamworld.

House at Ladphrao: two structures bordering an open deck, with gate, typical of old central Thai houses.

A Taste for Fantasy

The quest for fantasy is supremely Thai. You can see it in the glitter of the Grand Palace or Wat Pho, with their golden spires and the long thin *chofa* finials. It shows in the whimsy of royal villas such as Bang Pa-in just north of Bangkok, where a Chinese pavilion, a Buddhist temple built in the style of a Gothic church, and Thai palaces all co-exist in an oddly appealing whole.

In contemporary art, fantastical forms mark the work of Thailand's two most popular modern painters: Chalermchai Kositpipat and Thawan Duchanee. Chalermchai paints Dr Seuss-style trees waving swirling branches above multi-tiered palaces, whose rooflines twist and turn from Thai into Chinese and back again. Temples fly through pink and turquoise skies on the backs of birds and fish. In Thawan's darker vision, the curving forms of Thai design emerge from the black-outlined beaks and claws of ravenous animals. Not content merely to paint fantasy, Thawan constructed it in the grounds of his pleasure park far north in Chiang Rai – studios and showrooms on stilts, crowned with super-steep wooden roofs, and beams tipped with buffalo horns.

Chalermchai Kositpipat: eaves of Wat Rong Khun.

Thawan Duchanee (2005), seated on buffalo-horn chair.

One could say that a taste for fantasy is what decides whether a person is going to love Thai art or not. If your ideal is minimalism or conceptual art, Thailand will never satisfy. It's just too outlandish. For me, coming from years in elegant Japan, with the emphasis on simplicity, I found Thai exuberance a great release. My Sinologist friend Geremie Barmé, on hearing that I was moving to Thailand, said to me, 'You'll love it, Alex. Therapy! After Japan – Thailand is therapy!'

While the Ladphrao house was plain as Thai structures go, there were plenty of quirky fantasy touches, things you certainly wouldn't see in a modern apartment building – well, Thailand being what it is, maybe you would see them in a modern Bangkok apartment building. There were stone sculptures of frogs, gingerbread trellises and peacocks made of gilded foil perched over the doors.

Charming as all this may be, there was, of course, a reason for the reasonable rent. When Tom and I first took over, the houses were uninhabitable. The roofs leaked, there were no fans or air-conditioners, and the electrical wiring was completely baffling. The right wing of the Thai house had subsided into the soft ground below, so that the whole complex tilted to the side, like one of those cottages teetering on skewed pillars along the Nonthaburi Canal.

Thus began a long process of renovation, lasting for all the years that I rented the house. With the help of Khun Santi's carpenters from Ayutthaya, we jacked up the sunken right wing of the house. We replaced the timbers of the deck with hardwood planks, glazed the windows and installed air-conditioning, modern comforts that I, at least, can't live without. The electrician rewired all the buildings, and we installed lamps and spotlights. Gardeners brought the unruly garden under control, pruning branches and laying flower patches. In the end, as anyone who has restored an old wooden house could have foretold, Ladphrao turned out to be very expensive.

Partly because it took years before the house became habitable, I never actually lived at Ladphrao. From my condo in Sukhumvit, I commuted to Ladphrao for the occasional event or romantic evening. Sometimes I would go out there with friends and we would picnic on the central platform. We bought food at the local Chok-chai 4 Market, brought it back and ate by candlelight as rain swept over the wooden deck, accompanied by a chorus of frogs. Other times, as the moon rose from behind the fan palm, we watched a performance of traditional Thai dance.

The Empty Room

Seen from the perspective of Japan, Ladphrao felt familiar. The archetypal Japanese house came from Southeast Asia, not China. Old Japanese farmhouses are built of wood, raised up on stilts (although only a few feet, not a full storey like Thai houses), roofed with thatch or tiles and floored with polished wooden planks. Inside, open ceilings reveal exposed beamwork, and, despite having windows, somehow there's never enough light. All of which describes Khun Santi's houses to a tee.

Dance *sala* at Ladphrao: open-sided room with raised central floor, for relaxation and dance performance.

Another trait that Thailand shares with Japan is the lack of furniture. I call this the 'ethos of the empty room'. China and Korea filled interior spaces with furniture: chairs, tables, bookshelves and cabinets. But the Thai and Japanese tradition, even for the wealthy, calls for an open floor with little more than a mat and a cushion. I wonder sometimes what the effect of the 'empty room' had on people's psychology. Could it be related to the fact that both Japan and Thailand have focused so much on detachment and meditation?

Over time, Ladphrao saw many performances of dance and music. In this I felt a bond with Kukrit and Prince Naris, both of whom loved above all viewing dancers perform in their gardens and pavilions.

In Chinese ink paintings, if there is a cottage in the mountains, you can always peek through the window and glimpse a scholar with his books and writing brushes. Chinese architecture is just not complete without a resident philosopher.

Thai fantasy complexes, on the other hand, demand dancers, such as you might see within the palaces in temple murals. In using Ladphrao for dance performances, I felt I was turning the house to its truest use. Khun Santi once told Tom that when he came home at night and saw light emanating from the Thai pavilions, and heard the gongs and chimes of gamelan and the squeal of Thai oboes, he felt that the houses had come alive again.

One fact of old Thai houses is that the rooms are small. That's the main reason I spent many happy evenings, but never moved in to Ladphrao. There just wasn't enough

space to put all my things. The stark simplicity of traditional living in Thailand is something you wouldn't
suspect, guessing from vast halls of temples and palaces,
carved and painted over every inch and crammed with
Buddha statues. But these are where rituals took place,
not where people lived.

Jim Thompson's house, with its open-sided living
room, study, dining room and so forth, is misleading.
He put three or four houses together to craft his spacious mansion. Even royal residences in the past for
kings and queens were modest in size, as you can see
from the small palace Phra Tamnak Daeng (Red Mansion) in the grounds of the National Museum. Inside
these spaces, not much larger than a standard hotel
room, the mark of luxury for royalty would be a gilded
Chinese bed – and the rest was mostly empty. Most
striking was the small Thai villa that Rama V built for
himself in the gardens of his imposing colonial-style
Vinmanmek palace. (It was one of the largest teak structures in the world, but dismantled in 2018.) This little
house with its bare interior was where he went to relax.

Small, sparse rooms lend a mood of intimacy. King
Rama V was at his happiest when he had left his ladies to
formal tea in the plush Victorian drawing rooms of
Vimanmek, while he went to chat with friends in his little
bare cottage in the garden.

Ladphrao was no Shangri-La. It's not for nothing that
hundreds of millions of people, from Japan down to Java,
all decided in the last few decades to tear down their
charming wooden houses and rebuild in concrete and

plastic. The intimacy of the 'empty room' may be nice, but there comes a point when people crave space to put a refrigerator, magazines, tables and chairs. People once lived simply on the floor, and that was that. But with modern life, old houses feel cramped. And indeed they are. Ladphrao required constant 'object control'. Bring in one too many things and you found you had no room to move.

As in Japan, the eaves and doorframes were all too low. I was constantly cracking my forehead against something. Then there was having the bathroom located down a flight of stairs and across the courtyard. It's quite a trip to make in the middle of the night, and a bit scary if you're spending the night all alone.

Maintenance

The maintenance was endless. Bits and pieces from the trees rained down on the garden night and day, requiring constant sweeping. The restoration work never ended. The best we could do about the leaking roofs of the double-winged house was to cover them with green canvas. The steps rotted and had to be replaced, the house subsided some more, and the floor tiles cracked. The electricity shorted, the lower rooms flooded, the red paint flaked away in the hot sun, the gutters got choked with leaves. A huge branch fell off the banyan tree after a storm and smashed the fretted woodwork along a corner of the *sala*.

I experienced this in Japan with the thatched farm-house I bought in Iya Valley on the island of Shikoku in 1973. In those days, all the houses in the mountains of inner Shikoku were thatched. Every autumn, the villagers cut thatch and stored it; and in the spring they gathered to redo the roofs in sequence. As long as they kept doing it, the price was cheap and the process easy. However, once people stopped thatching roofs, a vicious circle set in. Thatch, which had been the most common thing in the world, became rare and ended up as a luxury. A similar process has happened in Thailand.

Houses like Khun Santi's were once easy to maintain because the materials and skilled craftsmen were plentiful. Nowadays, everything about these houses is 'special', and so the costs have skyrocketed. Old houses run so against the thrust of the city's new development that it's natural that their upkeep would be a challenge.

Yet, while the maintenance was unending, the house was the supreme place for dancers to perform. I've seen Thai dancers in many venues, but I really feel they need to be seen in the context of an old wooden *sala*, such as we had at Ladphrao, shaded by the great banyan tree. Sliding their feet over those smooth wooden floors, the masked dancers ceased to be human and became as Thai dance is intended to be: avatars descended to earth from paradise.

Originally, I had hoped to use the Ladphrao house as the centre for a programme of traditional Thai arts, and for a while it did serve that function. But the Thai arts programme took on more variety over time to fit the needs of our visitors, and we ended up hosting the pro-gramme as often as not at the houses of friends or at my apartment downtown. We used the complex less and less, and finally, in 2013 I handed the house back to Khun Santi. The door to my dream of living in an old Thai house shut behind me.

The amazing thing is that this house existed at all at the start of the twenty-first century in Bangkok. Thai houses always had something fantasy-like about them, and nowadays against the backdrop of the modern city, they feel all the more unreal, a mirage of a vanished life-style. Outside the walls of the house at Ladphrao, the busy, dusty city and congested highways stretch far and wide. Inside, orchids bloom under the sun-speckled shade of palms and the banyan tree, birds twitter, peaked roofs soar into a blue sky, and shadows drift over red-painted pavilions.

Ladphrao is now gone, but I did have those fifteen sweet years, and what more can you ask for in life? I was able to taste in reality all the pleasure of the dream.

Apartment 6
ชุมชนระฟ้า

เขตดาวน์ทาวน์

In Thai soaps, the rich dwell in a colonnaded mansion approached through cast-iron gates and a circular driveway lined with sculpted hedges. Inside a vast marble-floored living room, the family cowers at the feet of a fascinatingly evil mother-in-law with truly amazing hair. In real life, few people in Bangkok live in single-family homes these days, even the best-coiffed matriarchs. Bangkokians are moving into apartments in high-rise buildings, and as the levelling of old homesteads continues, the trend will surely endure. Bangkok has taken to the sky.

From the beginning, I have only ever properly lived in apartments. The first was a one-room apartment that I rented back in 1990. It was on Soi Rongnamkaeng ('Ice Factory Road') just off Sathorn, a *soi* so narrow that even tuktuks couldn't get down it. To get there, you had to alight from your taxi by a crowded market and then walk past a mosque, some walled compounds and empty lots with vines growing over wooden fences. About two hundred yards down this narrow lane rose a six-storey apartment block where I lived on the third floor. Although just off the roaring avenue of Sathorn, it had a relaxed feeling, like living in a small town. During the day children played in the *soi*; at night, people wearing sarongs sat outside in the cool of the evening, chatting.

It didn't last long. Word was out that the city had plans to build a new road through the market, although many of the shopkeepers and squatters refused to move. One morning, we woke up to find the whole market burned to the ground. Several people died in what the police determined was a 'tragic accident'. Soon thereafter, the road building began, and most of the district vanished.

After the burning of the market, I moved to another one-room apartment, this time on the fifth floor of dilapidated Indra Condominium, one of Bangkok's older large condos, behind the Indra Hotel in Pratunam.

In a colourful city, Pratunam must be one of its most colourful neighbourhoods. In the centre rise two skyscrapers: Baiyoke 1 and Baiyoke 2. When I moved to Pratunam, there was only Baiyoke 1, at the time Bangkok's tallest building, which had a restaurant at the top from which I would show guests the vastness of Bangkok spreading in a jumble of buildings to the horizon. Later, they built Baiyoke 2, nearly double the height of the first one, and with its elongated 'Empire State Building' shape, topped by a circular drum, it still towers as a landmark over central Bangkok.

At the ground level, these two buildings stand in the middle of a warren of small shops and shipping agents. It's Bangkok's busiest garment centre. Buyers with shopping bags cram the streets all day long, and these include not only Thais but wholesalers from all over the world. Russian babushkas cart off huge bags of T-shirts, almost as wide as themselves, for export to Uzbekistan. Nigerian ladies arrayed in yards of colourful fabric and regal head-dresses parade majestically through the streets, which also feature restaurants serving African favourites.

Pratunam was an easy place to live because you could go out on to the street at any time of day or night and buy food, cosmetics, flowers, just about anything. The neighbourhood brims with hotels, from five-star to cheap flophouses; there was every kind of eatery; and nearby they were converting a failed department store into Panthip Plaza, which in a few years became Bangkok's premier electronics emporium. There were certain disadvantages: notably our *soi* flooded so badly after heavy rains that I sometimes found myself wading home in knee-high, or even waist-high, water.

High-rise Living

The next move took me up into the sky. In 1996, a friend introduced me to Khun Num, a wealthy young philanthropist who lived in a condominium tower on Sukhumvit Soi 16. Just how wealthy Num was I could only guess from our first conversation, in which I asked, 'And what do you do?'

'Oh, I work with my family,' he answered.

'What do they do?'

'We buy and sell things.'

'What sort of things?'

'Airplanes,' answered Num. I asked no further.

Num owned two apartments, together making up one floor of the condo tower. He invited me to take over one of them – at a rent which was affordable. A rent, in fact, that would only be possible in Bangkok. I was getting ready to finally make my move from Japan to Thailand official and I needed a space large enough to store my books and art collection built up over the years in Japan. In 1996, I moved in, and in 1997, shipped everything from Kyoto. It was a joy to have space, for the first time in decades, for all my books, which I'd never been able to fit into Tenmangu, the paper-walled Japanese house where I lived in Kyoto.

I've learned that people rate art works according to the quality of your bathroom. In the early days in Tenmangu, city plumbing had not yet reached my neighbourhood, so visitors had to use a wooden outhouse in the back. Japanese guests would look at the folding screens, and ask, 'Where do you get this stuff? Out of old trash piles, I guess?' They didn't mean to be rude; in their eyes these things really looked like junk. Later, when plumbing arrived and I built a tiled bathroom with a flush toilet, guests looking at the same screens sighed, 'We can never find treasures like this in Japan any more. You must have bid for them at international auction at Christie's.'

At Soi 16, it's tall windows and wide floors that work the magic. Every bit of driftwood or a lacquer bowl that I picked up at the Chatuchak Weekend Market looks like a masterpiece. Space being the luxury of big cities, people assume that I must be a person of great wealth. They're unaware that what I pay to rent the condo at Soi 16 is a fraction of what people pay for cramped apartments in Tokyo. In Manhattan, I'd be able to afford, maybe, a broom closet. It's the cheapness of Bangkok real estate that makes it possible for someone like me to live the way I do. And I live in the uneasy understanding that these days are numbered.

Just below us is the floor with the pool. Lit up bright-blue at night, it floats on the twelfth-floor rooftop like an alpine lake in the sky, a cool refuge in this ever-hot city. I float on my back and gaze upwards at the night sky, framed by tall buildings on both sides. Sometimes we come down to the pool to watch fireworks. Bangkok must surely have more fireworks displays than any place on earth. It's the sense of *sanuk* that's so core to Thailand, expressing itself in constant celebrations.

The sky-floating pool represents an aspect of Bangkok, which is that even at great heights, there are outdoor

Soi 16 pool in the sky.

spaces open to the sky. In northern cities, chilly-to-freezing weather half the year is enough to make this unfeasible. In Singapore, safety concerns make it illegal. But in Bangkok, many a high-rise features a pool or recreation area on upper floors; and some boast rooftop restaurants at truly dizzying levels.

The most spectacular of such venues is Sirocco restaurant, located on the rooftop of the State Tower at the foot of Silom Road. You ride up to the sixty-third floor, then walk outdoors to the top of a broad flight of stairs. Your designer dress and styled hair swirling in stratospheric winds, you descend like a 1940s Hollywood star down the illuminated staircase to a candle-lit dining space, dark in the evening sky. At the end of the dining area is the bar, a circular extension aglow with changing rainbow colours, perched over the edge of nowhere. Far below snakes the curve of the Chao Phraya River, busy with river-craft, and all around gleam the lights of the sky-scrapers of new Bangkok.

For the first year or two, from the Soi 16 windows we had a view of the lake at Queen Sirikit National Convention Centre, although the office buildings going up in the pre-1997 boom were beginning to obscure it. Family compounds, complete with lawns and pleasure ponds, surrounded our building, and at night you could hear frogs croaking during the rainy season.

Today, the view is long gone. We're hemmed in by high-rises, the walled family estates disappeared one after another, and I haven't heard a frog in years. If there is any benefit to the loss of the view, it's that the new buildings shelter us from the blistering sunlight of a south-facing exposure. One welcomes almost anything for the blessing of shade.

Sky Train and Subway

The Soi 16 apartment stands a three-minute walk from Asok BTS sky train station. I date 'new Bangkok' from the opening of the sky train in 1999. It made it possible, for the first time, to jump over the horrific traffic of the city. The new ease of getting around made it possible to do much more in a day.

That ease of movement, however, created a whole new

Entrance to Asok (BTS) Sky Train Station.

class of busy commuters. I remember when Khajorn first visited Tokyo in 1994. He stood in the concourse of Tokyo station watching as tens of thousands of commuters tramped by and, appalled at the inhuman scale of it all, he sighed and said, 'I hope Thailand never becomes this way!' A few years ago, I was changing trains at Siam Station, and as I struggled through rush hour crowds, I thought, 'It's happened, just as Khajorn had foreseen.'

Part of the change was psychological. The existence of stations and train lines put bones and sinews into the geography of the city. Until then, we had only a vague idea of where we were. Now, people are quite precise about their location, and the time it takes to get anywhere.

Another side effect of the sky train was that it allowed us to see the city in a way we hadn't before. While riding in the elevated sky train you can see into gardens and estates that formerly stood invisible behind high walls.

The subway (MRT), which came along a few years later, is quite the opposite. You go underground, sit for a while, and pop up somewhere else. This too inculcates a sense of location. You've got to have a clear idea of where you are and where you're going, north, south, east, or west.

The problem is what happens when you do emerge from the subway. Then chaos sets in again. For example, the MRT station called 'Thailand Cultural Centre' exits a fifteen-minute walk from the Centre. From there you walk up a highway, around a corner and back again, across a roaring junction with no pedestrian crossing, manoeuvring through stretches of mud and rubble along the way. You see society matrons in high heels staggering over this obstacle course – which they could have bypassed in three minutes if there were a tunnel leading from the station to the Cultural Centre.

These are quibbles; we're lucky to have the sky train and the subway, and this became even more apparent when in 2019 the subway finally reached Rattanakosin Island, the historic centre. Until then, the traditional culture of the old city was isolated from the new. Venues like the National Gallery and the National Theatre, located in prime locations near the Grand Palace, withered on the vine. Now it's become much easier.

My Sukhumvit neighbourhood is an enclave for foreigners, and so we're surrounded by expat amenities: a

Foodland supermarket (open twenty-four hours) across the street, with its restaurant Took Lae Dee ('cheap and good'), crowded even at 3 a.m. in the morning; Kuppa restaurant, one of Bangkok's finest, just a block away; the Siam Society, an historic venue just north of the intersection, complete with a traditional northern Thai house in the garden; and Emporium, the posh shopping centre, one Sky Train stop away.

Our area features another type of expat amenity: Soi Cowboy, a street of go-go bars just off of Soi Asoke. Local expats frequent the red-light district of Soi Cowboy, as opposed to the better-known Patpong, which largely caters to tourists. Soi Cowboy is not something to be especially proud of, but it does lend a bit of colour to a relatively staid neighbourhood.

A market opens at noon on Soi 16 for the lunchtime crowd emerging from nearby office buildings. You can find a little clutch of food stands wherever there is a large construction site, and on this *soi* there has been no end to building. However, compared to the crammed alleys of Pratunam, there is relatively little street life around here. For better or for worse, it's a harbinger of the bland bourgeois Bangkok that's approaching.

Bland as it may be, there are many things to remind us, even in our glassy tower, that this is Bangkok and that the surroundings are Thai. To begin with, nobody goes in or out of our building without paying respects to the golden statue of Brahma enthroned in a tall white-plastered shrine. Instinctively people make the *wai* greeting as they walk past.

Win motersai: motorcycle boys with numbered jackets wait
for customers at the mouth of Sukhumvit Soi 16.

Just up from the shrine, at the mouth of the *soi*, lounge
a flock of motorcycle boys, dressed in monogrammed
jackets. The *soi* boys provide the solution for getting in
and out of deep side streets, because public transport
only covers the main avenues. Wearing jackets indicating
their neighbourhood, they lounge at *paak soi*, 'the mouth
of the *soi*', waiting for customers who need to be carried
inside the *soi*. They're known as *win motersai* (from the
English word 'win', it is said, because the customer

arriving soonest 'wins' the right to use a motorcycle boy's services).

Khlong Toei Slum

Despite the wealth of the neighbourhood, poverty is not far away. Only a few blocks south of our apartment building is Khlong Toei Market, adjacent to one of Bangkok's most notorious slums. My eighteen-year-old niece Tasi, Edan's more serious sister, spent six months working as a volunteer for a charity NGO based in Khlong Toei.

Tasi's first days were traumatic: they assigned her to the AIDS ward, where she came face-to-face with helpless patients dying in filthy hovels. Later she shifted to performing puppet shows for children, which was less stressful. Although Tasi found the children smiling and cheerful, the contrast between the air-conditioned comforts of Soi 16 and the odorous poverty of Khlong Toei was almost surreal. It's a reminder of another reality for foreigners living in Bangkok (certainly most Westerners and Japanese): huge income gaps.

Of course, they're huge in New York too. The difference is that here the poor and the rich still live cheek by jowl. My cousin Tom has explained the value of slums: they allow poor people to live in the city centre. In America, poor people's lives are dominated by the hours they spend commuting to the wealthy parts of town, where the jobs are. America has segregated rich from poor in its cities.

As Tasi saw, life in the slums is hardly easy. At the same time, visitors from abroad get a distorted view from the extensive literature on the living hell that is Bangkok's slums. There seems to be demand for this among foreign tourists, as there is for books by convicted drug smugglers describing the ghastly goings on in Thai jails.

In fact, slums in Bangkok are something of a success story. While as much as half of the populations in cities like Mumbai, Manila and Dhaka live in slums, only about 10–15 per cent do in Bangkok. Bangkok has a market of rental housing that reaches every corner of the city, offering rooms with rents cheap enough for even a low-paid labourer or market vendor to afford.

Bangkok has little land under control by public agencies. As the city expanded from swamp into mega-city, it has swallowed up rice paddies and durian orchards that were broken up into family-owned holdings. This development of Bangkok – in thousands of tiny bits instead of a few big chunks – has made for a planner's nightmare but a city of small-scale landowners.

Every mum and dad can rent out their bit of land to poor migrants to build shacks on, or develop a few rental rooms. If they've got more cash to invest, they can build a 3–4-storey building with one-room rental units, which is the city's low-income housing type.

Because Bangkok expanded into empty swamps so quickly, the city is full of pockets that the developers haven't yet concreted over: vacant lots, tin-roofed huts on stilts along the edges of marshes. Nestled in the shadow of modern towers, these are the nooks and crannies where the poor stake their claim.

Bangkok benefits from what Tom calls 'the culture of negotiation'. When conflicts arise between landowners and tenants or squatters, most pay little heed to the letter of the law, and instead work out a compromise. In Manila or Jakarta, landlords insist on the legal fact of their ownership, calling the police in with riot gear to brutally evict slum-dwellers.

In Bangkok, while there are painful exceptions, it's generally considered a loss of face to evict people from your land by using force. So Thailand has come up with an approach to housing for the poor. It capitalizes on the culture of negotiation, setting poor communities free to finagle their own land deals. If a slum occupies land facing a major road, the landlord might be persuaded to sell or rent part of the land cheaply to the community, if they agree to give him back the commercially viable part of the land along the main road. The owner can then make money on the road-front bit, and the people can rebuild their houses on this smaller piece of land behind it.

The National Housing Authority does build some large public housing projects, which are as prone to mismanagement here as in other cities around the world. But most of the upgrades take place inside of neighbourhoods, with residents cutting their own deals with landowners. That's why Bangkok has so many small two- or three-storey shop houses and apartment buildings, and is not dominated by the massive Soviet-style housing towers you see in a city like Beijing.

This process is to housing what the street stalls and Chatuchak Market are to business: small-scale, neighbourhood-oriented, flexible. It can happen because of the Thais' ability to negotiate.

Lurid writing about teenagers overdosing on drugs, children being raped in slums and so forth is part of the 'sexpot Babylon' approach that has given Bangkok such an unsavoury reputation. While drugs and crime certainly exist in Bangkok, these things happen in any big urban area. Tom remarks, 'People who live in slums are not some strange species living in a nightmare world. Because their jobs as construction workers, *som tam* ladies or masseurs don't pay enough, they're forced to live in a shack in a slum.'

Despite Bangkok's relatively humane approach to slums, sudden clearances such as the one that erased the ill-fated market of Soi Rongnamkaeng do sometimes happen. At the end of 2006, a portion of a slum neighbourhood – about fifty houses – just a block from my Soi 16 condo, went up in flames one evening. Other slums are better protected, with advocate committees and NGOs who fight for squatters' rights.

Although the bastion of the affluent, Sukhumvit mostly looks as shabby as the rest of the city. It's a matter of degree. You could hardly say that these are beautiful surroundings. Grimy shophouses line much of Sukhumvit, fronted by tangles of electrical wires hanging just over pedestrians' heads. Sometimes I look at the convolutions

Utility lines.

of those wires and muse how many lines are actually functional. Some day Bangkok will have to simply turn off all the lights, rip away the snaking, twisted wires and start over again.

The Great Jumble

Trees were once plentiful in Bangkok, but they've fared badly in recent years. There's hardly a tree in my neighbourhood that hasn't had branches lopped off because they interfere with the electric lines. Scraggly plants along the roadside seem doomed never to rise above a few feet before they too get lopped off; or they simply wither away from lack of proper tending.

The city administration has taken a hint from Japan, where trees are seen as 'messy' and 'dangerous'. Branches going every which way, and falling twigs and leaves, are unruly. They're emblems of 'anti-progress', deserving to be chopped down in their right, even if they don't inter-fere with utility lines or anything else. In April 2020, we woke up to find that the city had truncated a big stretch of its last bastion of shady trees, lining Wireless Road. Shadeless streets, Japanese-style, is where we're now headed.

Bangkok pavement is terrible. Even in fashionable Sukhumvit you really have to watch your feet, or you might stumble over a patch of rubble, or step into a drainage ditch. At the Asoke-Sukhumvit intersection, jagged metal signs veer over the sidewalk just at head level. Crossing the street can be a life-threatening experi-ence, since vehicles charge from all directions, sometimes even running against the traffic.

What all this adds up to is an all-enveloping chaos and ugliness. Tokyo too is ugly, but at least it's a sterilized clutter. Singapore is not only clean, but actually beautiful, with vast rain trees spreading their branches over the ave-nues of the downtown shopping district. However, with a few special exceptions, such as the Grand Palace area, Bangkok is just a mess. One wonders why this is so, given the Thais' love of cleanliness and the traditional social ideal of *riaproy*, which means 'proper', 'correct', 'everything in its place'.

Yet the city is an unrelieved jumble. Bangkok has a bad reputation abroad as a slummy, traffic-choked megalopolis. True, but one must keep in mind the fact that no modern Asian town is beautiful, with the exceptions of Singapore and parts of Hong Kong. Fragments of old city centres survive with much charm, as in Hanoi's Old Quarter, or Gion in Kyoto. But the new cities surrounding these are bleak conglomerations of blocky concrete buildings, power lines and clashing signage. Even Kyoto, beyond a few lovely central blocks, basically looks like *Blade Runner*.

Modern city planning – zoning, caring for trees, burial of utility lines, heritage preservation – is a 'technology' from the West. The British brought with them a tradition of civic administration to Hong Kong and Singapore that Bangkok never experienced. None of the other modern Asian cities – Seoul, Manila, Jakarta – have much visual charm. Beijing is the saddest case, as a ruthless administration has flattened the old town and replaced it with offices and apartments straddling massive plots fully a city block in size – bounded by avenues of eight or even ten lanes. The effect is of a kind of brutal grandeur – but you can walk for blocks without seeing so much as a cigarette stand.

Bangkok is thus not unique in being ugly. Tokyo and Beijing are, however, better organized. The filthiness, the rubble-filled roadways – these are the marks of a Third World country. Which is, after all, where we live.

Despite its growing wealth, Thailand has only recently risen from being a poor place. It's still the 'Third World'.

It creates for Bangkok an image problem. Foreign visitors are appalled at, even tormented by, the sex industry of Bangkok, but blissfully unconcerned with far larger sex businesses in other countries, such as India or Japan. The vibrant 'in your face' energy of Bangkok makes people think the city dirtier and more sinful than it really is.

As a 'Third World' country, Thailand comes rather high on the scale, far above most of its neighbours (Cambodia, Myanmar, Laos, Vietnam) in social infrastructure. Friends arriving back in Bangkok after a trip to India sigh with relief on arrival at efficient Suvarnabhumi Airport. Some aspects of the city are already well-advanced, such as the Sky Train and Subway, superior to public transport in many American cities. Over the next decades Thailand will cross the line that Korea and Japan long ago crossed, and become a 'developed country'. *Riaproy* will have its victory. But in the meantime, rubbley pavement, chopped-up trees and snarled wiring define the reality of Bangkok.

Beauty, we lack. Variety – no one else comes close. Even New York would be challenged to offer the variety provided by my neighbourhood: motorcycle boys, Brahma shrines, the bars of Soi Cowboy, stylishly dressed girls on the Sky Train, street markets at lunchtime, an old Thai house on stilts in the garden of the Siam Society, walled neo-colonial mansions wherein dwell evil matriarchs, grimy Chinese shophouses, swimming pools floating in the sky, Khlong Toei slum, glass and chrome skyscrapers. Sometimes the neighbourhood next door goes up in smoke; sometimes we have fireworks.

It's no paragon of aesthetics. But there's too much going on for anyone to care.

Origin 7
ต้นสายปลายเหตุ
เขตต้นตระกูลไทย

ne old friend, on hearing of my departure for Bangkok in 1997, asked with
genuine concern, 'How could you
leave Japan, with its depth and richness, for Thailand, where the culture is
so shallow?'

I understood the question, because I used to think the
same thing. Despite the fun I had in Bangkok in the
1970s, I never really thought of Thailand as having a culture on a par with Japan. My studies in China and years
of living in Japan entitled me, I thought, to call myself an
'East Asian cultural expert'. It was only after I made the

move to Bangkok in 1997 that I discovered that there was the huge world of Southeast Asia culture about which I knew simply nothing.

I travelled to Angkor in Cambodia and discovered sculpture which for its portrayal of the nobility of the human body could be compared with Greece, standing at a level far beyond anything ever produced in China. There may have been a Khmer statue or two in my text books, but why weren't these things discussed more seriously, recognized as sublime?

My friends in Bangkok collected Lao and Burmese textiles, revelling in weave techniques and patterns I'd never seen before. After hearing so much about Indonesia as one source of Thai culture, I finally visited Yogyakarta in Java. The exquisite elegance of the gamelan music and dance I saw in the Yogya royal court was nothing short of a revelation. These things were at a level of sophistication right up there with Kabuki or Noh drama – maybe surpassing them in their supernal beauty. How could I not have known about this? Why had I not gone to Java decades earlier?

All these cultures had influenced Thailand, which now began to reveal its complexity. 'East Asian cultural expert' was a sham, even a scam, if I didn't know about these things. Embarrassed at my ignorance, I went back to being a student, and I've been a student ever since.

People sometimes ask me, 'Why did you move to

Thailand and get so involved in Southeast Asia?' My answer is 'Embarrassment.'

The Legend of Langkasuka

One of the early friends I made on moving here was Zulki- fli Bin Mohamad, a Malaysian dance theatre artist. In his early thirties at the time, Zul was part scholar and part mischief-maker, stirring things up at an arts organization set up by the Southeast Asia member states to which he had been posted by the Malaysian education ministry.

Zul hails from Kelantan, the northernmost and most strictly Islamic state of Malaysia, but also the home of old arts and traditions now lost in the rest of his coun- try. At one point I made a trip with him to Kelantan, and we took a boat to an island in the delta where the last practitioners of Kelantan shadow puppets performed for us. This place, located on the delicate borderlands between Siam to the north and Malay/Javanese cultures of the south, had developed its own unique culture. Some puppets looked Javanese, with movable arms and long noses; others looked Thai, their heads crowned with Siamese-style spires.

From Zul I learned of the kingdom of Langkasuka, located in the narrow neck of the Malay Peninsula between what's now Malaysia and Thailand. Originat- ing in the sixth century, it saw its heyday at the court of

Shadow puppets in Kelantan.

Pattani in the seventeenth and eighteenth centuries. For hundreds of years Pattani acted as a crucial way-station, funnelling gamelan music, puppets and angelic dances, from Java in the far south, up to central Thailand.

Pattani paid tribute to the Ayutthaya and Bangkok courts, and it used to be that you could see small gold and silver trees which were sent in tribute on display at a little museum in the Grand Palace, now closed. In the nineteenth century, the colonizing British drew a line across the peninsula. North of that, the area around Pattani was absorbed by Siam, while other Malay states went to the British, becoming eventually part of the nation of Malaysia. That was the end of Langkasuka.

Most remarkable about this history is that it's so little known. Who has ever even heard the word: Langkasuka?

I tried to patch up the blank spots in my knowledge

of Thailand. But I've never lived in or visited any place where it is so difficult to get hold of the historical truth. Earlier rulers rewrote history at will, and the bureaucracy today goes right on creating myths to suit Thai nationalism and the tourist trade.

After the fascist period of the 1930s through the 1950s, when dictator Field-Marshal Phibul Songkhram set out to establish a new national identity, the myth-making picked up steam. One of the early steps in 1939 was to change the name of the country from Siam, which had been for centuries the name of the empire based in Ayutthaya and early Bangkok, to 'Thailand'.

The idea was to create an ethnically unified state (as was being fostered in fascist Germany and Japan at the time). For their favoured ethnicity, the generals chose the Thai (or Tai), whose tribes, trickling down from the northern valleys, had established the first capitals at Sukhothai and Chiang Mai in the thirteenth century.

From the later nineteenth century onwards, the royal government in Bangkok had been trying to forge a 'Thai' identity. In fact, the nation was anything but ethnically unified, consisting of a wide mix of peoples – Mon, Southern Muslims, Khmer, Lao, Chinese, Thai Lue and many others – but this made it all the more imperative, in the eyes of the generals, that people start to think of themselves as 'Thai'. 'Siam' was briefly reinstated for a few years at the end of the Second World War. But soon afterwards, Phibul and the generals returned to power and restored 'Thailand' as the name of the kingdom, and it has remained so ever since.

What could be more quintessentially Thai than the greeting *sawasdii*? But actually this too is something cooked up by Phibul in the late 1940s. The problem was that the Thais didn't have at that time an expression equivalent to the Western *hello*. Phibul took the Sanskrit-based *savasti* (a word implying 'everything in good order') changed the final *ti* (or *di*) to *dii* (meaning 'good') and came up with *sawasdii*, the greeting that we now think of as hallowed tradition.

Today the Thai state is putting an ever-stronger mark on the arts. Numerous offices wield fiat: the Fine Arts Department, the Ministry of Tourism, the Ministry of Culture, the National Identity Board and, for an Orwellian touch, the Cultural Surveillance Centre.

Totsakan Never Dies

As a sign of how the Ministry of Culture exerts control, in 2006 there was a contretemps when Somtow Sucharitkul, Bangkok's opera composer and musical genius, produced an opera, *Ayodhya*, based on the Ramayana epic, in which Ravana, the demon, dies on stage. After the founding of Bangkok, Kings Rama I and II rewrote the Indian Rama-yana in Thai format, calling it the Ramakien. Since then, certain 'extra-textual' rules have coloured the Thai version.

One of these requires that the death of the demon Ravana (called Totsakan in Thai) must never be shown.

It's believed that should Totsakan die on stage, evil will befall the Kingdom. Nothing could better illustrate the Thais' sense that neither the good nor the bad should have the final say. Totsakan never dies. As we often read in the news about a political or army leader who has fallen from grace, he's just 'transferred to an inactive post'. The history of Thai coups and business scandals has shown that the bad guys never completely disappear.

In Somtow's case, the government forced him to restage the opera. At the climactic moment, the wounded Totsakan dragged himself off to die invisibly (although, this being opera, not inaudibly) in the wings.

It's hard to think of another country where the

Totsakan: the Demon King of the Ramakien epic
has bulging eyes, tusks and ten heads.

traditional arts have such a political dimension. In Japan, things like tea ceremony and Kabuki are well and truly irrelevant to the bureaucrats and even to the Imperial Family, whose involvement in culture is minimal.

In Thailand, on the other hand, the Ramayana's story of divine kingship underlies the monarchy – and plays a political role to this day. It goes back to the fourteenth-century Ayutthaya kingdom, which took its name from the mythical capital of the Ramayana in India, Ayodhya. A number of Ayutthaya kings had Rama, the hero, as part of their names, and the kings of the present Chakri dynasty of Bangkok continue to be called Rama.

Rama is an avatar of the Hindu god Vishnu (called Narai in Thai), whose mount is the divine bird-man Garuda. Narai graces royal temples and palaces, and the winged Garuda tops government documents and buildings. In Bangkok, we have roads and bridges named for the kings from Rama I to Rama IX. In short, the Ramayana epic is not just a performance, it's an affair of state.

The Thai government ever since Phibul Songkhram has been building up a national identity, leading to an obsession with 'Thai culture' that shapes the look of Bangkok. 'Thainess' lies in curving filigree and sparkling decoration, heavenly maidens wearing golden crowns, rising temple eaves, the prayer-like *wai* greeting.

The new Suvarnabhumi Airport was not deemed complete until it had installed a sculpture of Thai gods and goddesses cavorting in a purple, green and pink panorama of *The Churning of the Sea of Milk*. It's a scene from a Hindu creation myth in which the gods and demons pull

on a vast snake entwined around a mountain to churn the
nectar of immortality from the Sea of Milk. The original of
this image is carved along the gallery of Angkor Wat in
Cambodia, not in Thailand, but never mind.

The airport version is always crowded with people taking their final souvenir photo of Bangkok before they fly
out. You will not find such a strong cultural reminder in
the airports in Beijing or Tokyo. Similar visions greet you
as installations in hotels, shopping malls and banks. The
effort to be Thai is accelerating. The earliest bridges in
Bangkok looked 'Beaux Arts' European; later ones 'international industrial'. However, the newest bridges over
the Chao Phraya River were designed to appear notice-
ably Thai, such as the the Bhumibol Bridges in the
southeast of the city. With suspension cables flaring outwards from Thai-style pinnacles – they're part of a
cityscape that is distinctly Thai.

Bhumibol Bridges: the towers are topped with spires derived from *chedi*
(pagodas) and *chadaa* (crowns).

The Churning of the Sea of Milk: installation at Suvarnabhumi Airport depicting Vishnu atop the mountain, while gods and demons churn the nectar of immortality.

Despite all this, it's difficult as a traveller to experience real traditional culture in Bangkok. It's a pan-Asian problem.

Foreigners come to Japan or Thailand and would love to know something about the traditional arts. It's easy to see a show. But it's hard to hear an explanation that makes sense. You ask the Japanese tea master, 'Why did you turn the bowl first to the right and then to the left?' and he answers, 'Because that's the rule of the Urasenke School.'

Which leaves you back where you were before, namely baffled.

In Bangkok, what are we supposed to get out of the excruciatingly slow poses of Khon? If you don't know this, after the initial pleasure in the glittery costumes wears off, it's boredom. That's the unspoken truth of most people's introduction to Thai or Japanese arts: lovely, but what's the point?

Actually, many visitors to these countries would like to touch the inner wellsprings. However, it turns out that answering a question like 'Why did you turn the bowl in that way?' is not so easy.

The Collapse of Traditional Asia

It connects to how societies such as Japan and Thailand have adapted ancient ideas about how to live. Every country in the world wrestles with these things, but in the West we have it easy because so much of what people take for granted as 'modern' came out of our own history. Here in Asia it all arrived from somewhere else, and quite suddenly.

The result has been cultural collapse. While we hear a lot about 'Asian values', this disguises the degree to which Asian cities and countryside were transformed in the twentieth century. Mao and his heirs tore down the great walls of Beijing and, while preserving the Forbidden City and a few blocks of old neighbourhoods, they razed most of the rest. Old buildings may be quaint, but it's the new skyscrapers and boulevards that proclaim the nation's wealth and mastery of Western technology.

Bangkok too has changed unrecognizably, bearing little resemblance to the water city it once was. Outside of Rattanakosin (the old town with palaces and temples), it mostly consists of concrete shop houses, high-rise towers and billboards. Even Kyoto, beyond the walls of the Zen temples, looks like any other Japanese city: a conglomeration of squareish building blocks. Nothing remotely like this happened to Rome, Paris or Florence.

A few air pockets like Bali and Bhutan miraculously survived. But generally speaking the changes in East Asia were drastic – far beyond anything we can imagine in the pampered West.

In the West, we had hundreds of years of industrial

revolution and revolt against the Church and feudalism – and in the process old culture adapted itself to become new. It happened so slowly that most of us would hardly think that our present-day societies have a traditional base. Jeans and running shoes trace back to trousers and footwear worn by peasants in medieval Europe. The forms of our libraries, universities and theatres have changed little in five hundred or even two thousand years.

In contrast, there's hardly any aspect of modern life that emerged from within Asia; the thrust of it came from the West. Hence foreign photographers love to take 'old-together-with-new' images: a boy riding a water buffalo while speaking into a mobile phone; an orange-robed monk on a motorcycle. If it were Europe, we wouldn't be so fascinated by a farmer on his phone, or a priest on his bike. It's because it's Asia that these things appear to be so incongruous.

China, proud of being the 'Central Kingdom', found to its shock at the end of the nineteenth century that it was no longer central. China was out of date in every way, and the new world was dominated by the West and newly empowered Japan. The response was agonizing. China went through a paroxysm of destruction that has gone on for over a century and is still not at an end. It reached a high pitch in the Cultural Revolution in the 1960s, when Mao made every effort to wipe out the old civilization.

As we head into the 2020s, a new cultural revolution, backed by technologies of surveillance, is headed towards the final crushing of the past. Many of China's Buddhist and Daoist temples have already been commandeered to serve the policies of the Chinese Communist Party. In a weird historical twist, people wanting to study Chinese Buddhism or Daoism will not be able to learn much of value by going to China. The challenge for East Asian countries was how to save old things in their own cultures and give them new vitality in the modern day. To everyone's surprise, China, the richest culture of them all, might end up failing the test.

Japan was luckier. Unlike China, Japan kept its emperor, and early success as an imperialist power made the country proud of itself. Starting in the 1920s and 1930s, artists began a process of updating the tradition which goes on today. Yet Japan suffered a huge setback with the loss of the Pacific War. So drastic was the shock of the war (pre-war ideology rested on the idea that Japan was 'divine' and could never lose) that the public responded by rejecting everything old.

By the early 2000s, Japan was thoroughly urbanized, the Emperor relegated to the margins. Old cities were torn down and rebuilt; the countryside covered with concrete – and in this still-ongoing process the physical context of the culture was transformed almost beyond recognition. Nevertheless, the Emperor did survive, and so did Zen, Shinto, tea ceremony, which continue to live on behind walls in genuine settings of mossy temples and Kyoto gardens.

Thailand also was lucky, keeping its king, its religion and traditions of politeness and respect, as well as dress and architecture. But, as in Japan, the old ways of life are fast disappearing.

Living here in the midst of the great East Asian melt-down, you learn to let go. Nobody can save the physical remnants – old towns or landscapes – which have already disappeared or been hugely changed. The answer is to find the spiritual ideas that remain.

Seeking the Origin

That was the aim of the school of traditional arts we used to run at Oomoto in Japan. We tried to go beyond the rules of tea ceremony and so forth and 'return to the origin'. The word Oomoto means the 'Great Origin'. Inspired by that, I decided to call my Thai arts programme the 'Origin Programme'.

But in Bangkok, the ideals at the 'origin' were hard to define, because the arts of Thailand are such a hybrid. You have the input from Java, Myanmar and the other neighbours, and then, in the nineteenth century, Thailand's kings westernized their country as fast as they could, bringing in Italian neo-classical domes, along with British table manners and German railways. All this got mixed up with Thai tradition, and the mixing just continues.

Thais are proud to say that their country, unique in Asia, was never colonized, and this is largely true (excepting the wartime Japanese occupation). It makes a big difference because, unlike Myanmar, Thailand kept its monarchy, and unlike China and Korea, Thailand kept a solid faith in Buddhist religion, and it also kept its village life.

A high percentage of Bangkokians – likely the majority – hail from the countryside. Many an immaculately dressed young lady or stylish young man on the Sky Train came to the city from 'up-country' and until only recently played in the rice paddies with water buffaloes. They still might play in the rice paddies on holidays, when they go home to visit their parents and cousins. None of my staff at Origin are Bangkok-born. They return to the village regularly, and come back to the city laden with mangoes and fermented fish. Traditional life lies close to the surface.

There's a tendency in Bangkok, as there is in all great capital cities, to look down on everyone else as country yokels from the provinces. This dismissive attitude has resulted in decades of unrest since 2000 between the supporters and enemies of Prime Minister Thaksin and, more recently, between the army and the supporters of democracy.

So the problem is not just that of figuring out 'Thailand, versus neighbouring countries'. It's figuring out 'Bangkok versus the rest of the country'. Official 'Thainess', as we see it in Bangkok, with its gold curlicues and Khon masks, is just one form of Thai culture. There are many others – including the popular culture of the Bangkok streets, which is also left out of official 'Thainess'.

There's yet another side of Thai culture – it's the degree to which it relates to all of Asia, to all peoples – its universal value.

My friends in Japan couldn't understand what South-east Asia had to offer, but the big irony is that Japan's culture itself rests as much on Southeast Asia as it does on China. When the Japanese philosopher Okakura Tenshin penned his 1904 book *The Ideals of the East*, he opened with the phrase: 'Asia is One.' A thousand years ago the same form of Buddhism held sway from Borobudur in Java, across China and Korea, all the way up to Nara in Japan. Borders were more fluid, and races mixed freely.

Even now, despite all the later divisions, attitudes survive across East Asia that are as linked as they were in the eighth century. All across East Asia, you find varied forms of dance. The sultans of Yogyakarta prefer a softer, flowing mood, the dancers swaying as though floating on waves of the south seas. In contrast, Khon in royal Bangkok has a static quality. All action comes to a stop as the actors pose in a tableau, still as a temple wall painting. In Bali, dance is frenetic: hands trembling and twitching, eyes rolling. An electric thrill runs through Balinese dancers from start to finish.

The differences are obvious enough. More interesting are the similarities: curved-back fingers, painted faces, the blurring of lines between male and female, the idea that these are not humans but gods and goddesses dancing – this goes all the way up from Bali to Thailand, and then to Japan. Asia really is One.

In 2006, we opened up the Origin Programme for Thai Arts. The concept was to give, in a seminar lasting just a day or two, an introduction to the essential 'origin' of Thai arts. It wasn't aimed at arts experts or specialists;

students were mostly Western or Japanese travellers and residents. The teachers were Thai masters whom I'd come to know in my explorations into dance, music and so forth.

We began by offering programmes in the old Thai house in Ladphrao. Thirty years had passed since I first came to Thailand as a student in 1975; nearly ten years had gone by since my official move to Bangkok in 1997. It was the end of decades of study.

In that, I was wrong. It was not an end but a beginning. I thought the Origin Programme existed to teach visitors, but it was, in fact, to teach me.

I have to admit it: I fell for the Thai smile. It started at the airport on my return to Bangkok in 1989. The customs official glanced at my passport, said 'Good-looking man,' and smiled. The boy at the door of the hotel smiled. The waitress in the restaurant smiled. I was hooked.

Which puts me in the same box as millions of foreign tourists, bewitched by the cliché of the 'Thai smile'. Nothing in the world charms like the open, heart-melting sweetness of a Thai smile – and that is simply a fact.

Since the smile was my beginning with Thailand, we

begin the Origin Programme with the smile too. We're probing the origins of that smile, and they lie in *marayaat*, 'etiquette'. In the West, the word 'etiquette' sounds fussy and old-fashioned, carrying the feeling that it's to do with crooking your little finger when drinking tea – the sort of thing that's nearly irrelevant to most Europeans or Americans today. However, it's crucial in Thailand, to the extent that I would say that in Thailand, *marayaat*, not dance or painting, is the queen of the arts.

Etiquette and rituals of respect are not unique to Thailand and can be found across East Asia. Senior and junior, commoner, monk and king – everyone should be in their proper place. That's the idea behind the Thai greeting *sawasdii*, since its root word, *savasti*, derives from the swastika. The perfectly balanced arms of this ancient Hindu symbol imply that 'everything is in order'.

Japan also developed a cult of *reigi saho* ('rituals and ways of doing things'), which reaches its height in the rules of tea ceremony. In modern Japan, you find *reigi saho* everywhere: how high or low to bow to someone, or which seat the visitor should take on entering a corporate meeting room.

In Thailand *marayaat* spreads its tentacles deep into the society. Schools teach *marayaat* to grade school students; you can buy manuals and posters showing how to sit, stand or make the prayer-like *wai* greeting.

The Wai and the Kraab

Central to it all is the *wai*, a gesture of respect that came from India. Depending on whom you talk to, the *wai* symbolizes either a lotus bud or the peak of Mount Meru. The Thais took this gesture of two hands clasped together and then embellished it, creating four basic *wai*, depending on the relative social positions of those offering them.

The junior person *wais* first as a sign of respect, and then the senior *wais* in acceptance. However, monks *wai* nobody, not even the King, because, as members of the Buddhist Sangha (community of monks), they stand highest on the scale of respect.

The *wai* is just the beginning. There are ways to receive and give things, a way to walk in front of a senior person, and so forth. In very formal situations, the *wai* is subsumed into a *kraab*, or prostration, in which the offerer lies outstretched on the floor with hands reaching in front of him.

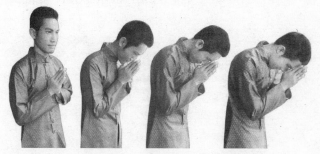

Four kinds of *wai*: (*left to right*) receiving a *wai*; *wai* to an equal; *wai* to a superior; *wai* to a monk or respected elder.

When Japanese come to Bangkok and study *marayaat*, they find Thai rituals familiar as just another form of *reigi saho*. For Westerners, however, they come as a surprise, because the easy Thai smile fools people into thinking that there are no rules. In fact, rules and consequences for ignoring them make Bangkok a serious place. For all its ethos of *sanuk*, people spend a lot of energy figuring out how best to act in the social hierarchy. Even the young staff members in my company address each other as 'younger', 'older', and so forth, though their age differences may be only a year or two.

This, of course, is not unique to Thailand, since paying attention to age differences, and using words like 'aunty', 'grandpa' and 'older brother' can be found across Asia. But Thailand carries this much further than most of the others. In any case, in *marayaat* there can be no such thing as 'equal'. One must be higher and the other lower.

For Thailand, this results in behavioural patterns, such as the 'patron–client relationship' commented upon by sociologists. The higher, more powerful figure

Kraab: prostration with one leg folded under the other, head to the floor and hands in a *wai*.

132

(the 'patron') bestows favour on a lower and dependent person (the 'client'). As foreigners living here, we would often wish for a more equal relationship with the Thais around us. But the grammar of the language works against that.

The Siamese kingdoms of central Thailand, culminating in Bangkok, inherited all the ritual of the Angkorian court. Plus, they devised a far-reaching system of ranking the citizenry, called *sakdina*. *Sakdina* was a measure of rank, denominated in *rai* (an acreage of rice fields). Japan had almost exactly the same system during the Edo period, which graded samurai according to their rice entitlement in bushels.

Siam carried *sakdina* much further than Japan did. In Japan, the system only applied to samurai, who accounted for 5 per cent of the population or less. In Siam, *sakdina* covered almost everybody, including Buddhist monks, housewives and Chinese merchants.

Rankings were: a slave, 5; a peasant, 25; a craftsman, 50; lower officials, 50–400. Above 400 were the ruling officials and nobility, the *khunnang*, rising up to ministers of state at 10,000.*

As the nation modernized in the nineteenth century, *sakdina* declined, becoming more symbolic than real, but it was only officially abolished in the coup of 1932. With the memory of *sakdina* so recent, the effects on people's psychology still show today. People are acutely

---

* David K. Wyatt, *Thailand: A Short History* (Hong Kong: Silkworm Books, 1984), p. 73.

aware of fine, even razor-sharp differences in their relative social status.

Becoming a *Phudii*

In the new society of the early twentieth century, the concept of *phudii* (meaning literally 'good people') took root in the cities, especially Bangkok, with its growing middle class. *Phudii* means 'decent people', 'ladies and gentlemen', with an implication of 'high class' versus 'low class'. In 1903, a book of proper manners was published called *Sombat Khong Phudii* (The Qualities of Decent People), which came to have immense influence. It's the first manual of *marayaat* as we know it today and, over a century later, still in print.

Sombat Khong Phudii consists of ten chapters, such as 'Maintaining Loveable Manners' and 'Possessing Grace'. It verged on a philosophy, describing each *phudii* quality in terms of 'action' (how to sit or walk), 'words' (what to say) and 'mind' (how to think).* To this day, even for people who haven't read it, *Sombat Khong Phudii* stands as a symbol of proper behaviour.

Phibul Songkhram, military dictator during the 1930s to the 1950s, launched a second wave of 'manner control'. Phibul tried to modernize Thailand's customs, dictating that ladies should wear hats, and husbands and

---

* Supawadee Inthawong, '*Sombat Khong Phudii*: A Century-old Tale on Manners Is Animated for Television Screens', *Bangkok Post* (25 September 2008).

wives were supposed to kiss each other when leaving for work in the morning. This set the pattern for the government telling people how to behave, which endures today.

People who write about Bangkok love to talk about how zany and chaotic it all is. However, the emphasis really should be on *riaproy* (propriety) and being a good *phudii*.

The gentleness that makes Thai life seem so attractive arises from the fact that people are taught from childhood to walk and speak softly and, above all, never to forget *krengjai*, 'reserve', or 'consideration'. 'Reserve' hardly covers the complexity of *krengjai*, which requires that one speak indirectly so as never to offend, take precautions so that others don't lose face, avoid becoming obligated, and never impose oneself. Thais walk and think with care. With the smile smoothing over all.

Thailand's iconic ancient text is the Traiphum (Three Worlds) cosmology written according to tradition by King Lithai of Sukhothai (reigned 1347). The Traiphum describes a hierarchy of three spiritual realms, expanding outwards in the physical world, and upwards in the spiritual realm. M. R. Chakrarot Chitrabongse, grandson of artist-prince Naris, declares: 'The Traiphum is the supreme conceptualization of the Thai people.'*

According to the Traiphum, thirty-one levels in three worlds revolve around the central axis of Mount Sumeru (also called Mount Meru). In our world, there are four continents, and seven rings of mountains between the four continents and Mount Sumeru. Each being finds

---

* Conversation with M. R. Chakrarot Chitrabongse at Oxford and Cambridge Annual Dinner, 7 October 2009.

ไตรภูมิ
Traiphum
Three Worlds Cosmology

Nirvana
นิพพาน

16 Divine Tiers
พรหม 16 ชั้น

Arupa Phum

World beyond Form

The Void
สูญญากาศ

Rupa Phum

World of Form

The Void
สูญญากาศ

Mt Sumeru
เขาพระสุเมรุ

Sun สุริยัน

Moon จันทรา

North Continent
อุตตรกุรุทวีป

Abodes of Gods
วิมาน

Himmaphan Forest
หิมพานต์

Seven Rings
of Mountains
เขาสัตตบริภัณฑ์

West Continent
อปรโคยานทวีป

East Continent
บุพเพวิเทหทวีป

Cosmic Ocean
สีทันดร

Cosmic Wall
กำแพงจักรวาล

Kama Phum

World of Sensuality

South
Continent
ชมพูทวีป

Hot Hells นรก

Cold Hells อเวจี

Anond Fish

ปลาอานนท์

Sketched by Vithi Phanichphant   วาดโดย อาจารย์วิถี พานิชพันธ์

his place in one of the many levels according to the
merit he has achieved in the cycle of rebirth. It's a well-
ordered system, and the fact that the Traiphum survived
the rise and fall of many dynasties shows that it appealed
to something deep in the Thai psyche – or at least, the
Thai rulers' psyche.

You can see the way even small things are organized in a detail such as the numbered jackets of motorcycle-taxi drivers. You sense the strength of authority in photos of politicians arrayed in pure white uniforms overlaid with sashes and decorations. If involved in academia and the arts, you'll learn how heavy the hand of orthodoxy lies upon them. Hard times befall people who dare to question the system.

At the Sky Train ticket window, people queue. Compared to Jakarta, Manila or even Shanghai, Bangkok has a low level of street crime. This means that, as in Tokyo, one can walk around most parts of the city in day or night and feel reasonably safe. It's not accidental, perhaps, that both Japan and Thailand fell into military rule in the early twentieth century (and in Thailand it continues right into the 2020s). Both had a history that disposed people to know their place and to follow the rules.

One of the unexpected twists of the Covid-19 pandemic in 2020–21 was the strong social cohesion of Thailand during the crisis. The majority of people wore masks without being told to do so, while public transport and restaurants rapidly installed social distancing. The Thais, to everyone's surprise, showed a discipline far beyond the supposedly well-behaved Japanese. Japan, in contrast, was lax and disorganized in its initial response, with the result that Thailand succeeded in controlling the virus with far more success than Japan, and indeed the rest of the world. The myth of 'happy-go-lucky Thais' needs to be retired.

Another thing happened during the Covid-19 crisis: with everyone wearing masks, the very font and base of Thailand's appeal – the Thai smile – disappeared. Or so one would have thought. And yet the smile somehow penetrated right through the masks. At the supermarket, the look from the woman tending the cash register had the same charm it always had. It turns out that the sweetness of the Thai smile doesn't lie in teeth and lips. It comes out through body language, through a tone of voice, through the eyes.

If one were to draw a difference between Japan and Thailand, it would be the effortless ease with which the Thais practise their etiquette. It all looks so natural that, unless someone points it out, you could easily fail to notice that there are four types of *wais*.

The paradigm of this style of 'effortless ease' is the formal Thai way of sitting, with legs folded under the body,

Thai and Japanese formal sitting posture: (*left*)
Thai *nang phap-phiap*; (*right*) Japanese *seiza*.

but slightly sideways, called *nang phap-phiap*. Elegantly off-balance, *nang phap-phiap* looks so much more informal than *seiza*, the Japanese sitting posture, which is firmly vertical, with legs folded directly back under the body.

Just looking at someone sitting *seiza* can make you feel uncomfortable. But try sitting the Thai way for any length of time. *Nang phap-phiap* is much harder on the back, even excruciating. You never would have guessed it from the look of relaxed poise.

Thai Grace

Nobody really knows who the original 'Thais' are, as they trickled down over millennia from the highlands of Vietnam and the mountains of southern China, and then merged with the Mon, Khmer and other indigenous peoples of the lowlands. This mix of races came up in the process with a quality that nobody else has.

I call this 'Thai grace'. Somehow, in the melting pot within which Thai culture formed, was distilled a tendency to swerve and elongate, prizing the feminine over the masculine, smoothness, polish. In social interactions you see it in the seamless grace of the way people greet each other, sliding in and out of a *wai* almost imperceptibly. Even a virile sport like Thai kickboxing begins with a swaying dance, the *wai khru*, 'paying homage to the masters', a world away from the thrusts of Chinese martial arts or the stomps of sumo.

The movements of *marayaat* all partake of this sway. Unlike the Japanese bow – up-and-down in a straight vertical motion – a *wai* is a swirl of interlinked curves. The elbows turn and fingers bend in alignment with a slight curve of the neck.

The exquisite curves of *marayaat* arose from the royal court. Somehow – perhaps it trickled down through the *sakdina* system – courtly refinement made its mark across society, right down to the village level. Even in peasants who've hardly been out of their hamlets in Isarn (the northeastern hinterland bordering Laos and Cambodia) or the North, you can see a natural grace of movement that parents have inculcated into their children.

Marayaat gives the Thais a 'vocabulary of elegance', which is denied to their brothers and sisters from other Asian nations who lost their royal courts. Some years ago, I went to Helsinki to attend an Asian Theatre Festival. There were a troupe of Myanmar dancers and Bangkok puppeteers. We went to visit the historical mansion of a local Finnish notable, and when we entered the reception room to take a commemorative photo, the Bangkok group formed themselves into a charming tableau, some reclining in princely repose on chairs, others with their legs crossed sideways on the floor in the style of *nang phap-phiap*. It had beauty, a sense of period, and wit. Sadly, the Myanmar dancers simply didn't know what to do with a room like this. The British deposed Burma's king over a century ago, and a military dictatorship repressed arts and culture since the 1960s.

In my travels I've never come across a society as gentle

as this one – on the surface. Thailand has its terrible injustices and shocking upheavals, such as the massacres of protestors in the 1970s and early 1990s. Thousands of people have died since 2000 in the troubles of the far south. Everyone knows about Thailand's poverty and prostitution, to the extent that foreign journalists focus heavily on these issues. Desperate slums, gangsters, brutal prisons – this place is no paradise.

That has been underscored in the unrest since the mid-2000s (and continuing), which reached its height with the struggle between the Yellow Shirts (opponents of exiled Prime Minister Thaksin) and the Red Shirts (Thaksin's supporters). In the summer of 2008, the Yellow Shirts occupied the grounds of Government House for 193 days. I went to Government House one day to see what was going on. Far from political mayhem, the Yellow rally struck me as closer to a *ngan wat*, a temple fair. People strolled down lanes lined with food stands and stalls selling anti-Thaksin hats and of course yellow shirts. At night bands would play, and people got up to dance.

Half a year later, the Red Shirts adopted similar tactics. The mood was still basically festive and, given the turmoil of the times, remarkably peaceful.

During this period of unrest, the striking thing about the rallies of both sides was the feeling of *sanuk*. There was lots of humour and dancing. Nevertheless, in both cases there was also an undercurrent of menace, and at times it broke through to violence. As the grand finale, in May 2010, the army cracked down on the Red demonstrations, resulting in thousands of injuries and dozens of deaths. The Reds on their part sent large parts of the city up in flames.

With an interlude from 2011 to 2014, the army has been in control ever since. In the summer and autumn of 2020, a new generation of demonstrators, mostly college and high-school students, once again flooded the streets demanding a return to democracy. Opposed to military rule, they also dared to question the role of the monarchy.

This time coloured shirts – now a thing of the past – were absent, as the youth groups do not affiliate with any one political party. Whimsy and *sanuk* reappeared in the pop-culture symbols chosen by the students: the three-finger salute from the movie *Hunger Games*, and a song from a Japanese anime *Hamtaro* about a hamster running around and around on his wheel. The students changed the words of the *Hamtaro* song from 'the most delicious food is sunflower seeds' to 'the most delicious food is taxpayers' money'.

Despite the students' exuberance, by the spring of 2021 most of their leaders were under arrest, the protests largely quashed. Until next time. So it would be a big mistake to just focus on the *sanuk*. Beneath the colourful surface run strong undercurrents of anger and bitterness. Thailand's struggles will continue.

This trauma is the dark side of the Thai moon, and it underlies much of contemporary art, which focuses on social injustice, grief and anger. Nevertheless, the day-to-day style of ordinary human contact is uniquely soft.

After living for a while in Bangkok, a visit to Beijing or New York jars the senses. The decibel level of daily conversation has gone up several notches – everywhere, strident voices assault the ear.

In its love of the placid surface, Thailand stands close to Japan. Both languages contain a wealth of polite words to indicate who is higher and lower, more intimate or more distant, and so on. To speak without them is to be not only rude, but ungrammatical, even unintelligible. The bowing and politeness is one of the things that wins people's hearts when they visit Japan.

Move on to India or the Middle East, and the level of pressure in human encounters ratchets up another notch. You don't easily get through the day in these countries with just a *wai*, a bow, or a smile.

As for us Americans and Europeans, we insist on our individuality, and whether we intend to or not, we can go too far. Conversation can be bruising, interactions brusque. My Thai staff chides me about how quickly I eat, or how loudly I walk, even in my own home. *Bao-bao*, they say, meaning 'softly!' It's one of the first lessons that Thais learn as children: *bao-bao*. I'm told that it arose from old Thai wooden houses, where the creaking floors registered every slight footfall. From this grows the idea that humans walk lightly; *yak* (demons) and *phii* (ghosts) are noisy things that go bump in the night.

On the chaotic Bangkok streets, as people commute to the office or go shopping, each Thai carries with him or her a whiff of the perfume of gentleness. The Thais bring grace to the surface of daily life, in a way that few

143

other peoples could match, and this helps to explain the otherwise inexplicable appeal of Bangkok, a far from attractive city.

There are, of course, exceptions to the rule of gentleness. New visitors complain that taxi drivers can be quite aggressive in steering the hapless rider to a tailor shop or jewellery store. In fact, Bangkok does seem to be the home of many bold and ingenious scams aimed at foreign travellers.

Wondering how this happens in a country devoted to politeness, I think of anthropologist Ruth Benedict's explanation for how the proper and polite Japanese could carry out the Nanking Massacre. Writing in 1946, Benedict argued that the rules of decorum only applied to Japan; other people were aliens, and thus soldiers in China found themselves with no rules at all, and they went crazy. In Thailand, much of the rudeness and scamming seems aimed at freshly arrived foreigners. That is, at people who stand outside the Thai hierarchies.

However badly they may be fleeced in diamond shops, Westerners and wealthy Asian visitors from countries like Japan get great treatment in contrast to poor immigrants from Burma, Laos and Cambodia. Periodically the newspapers reveal horror stories, such as the reports in 2009 that Burmese migrants were reputedly put on boats without food or water and floated out to sea.

Plenty goes on that doesn't give much to smile about, and yet the Thai smile remains a social reality. Some years ago, one Thai academic came up with the idea of 'cultural capital', meaning the ability to make money from selling culture, and of course the biggest 'cultural capital' Thailand has is the cult of gentleness. Each time a doorman or waiter charms a visitor with an unaffected smile and a *wai*, Thai grace is making itself felt.

Commentators in Bangkok newspapers wring their hands that Bangkok will lose out to Singapore or Shanghai as an international hub because of poor infrastructure or its backward educational system. Those are serious concerns. But Bangkok will always have something that neither Singapore nor Shanghai could ever provide, and it's the sheer niceness of daily life. That will continue to make this city a place that foreigners will want to visit, to live and to set up businesses.

Danger Signs

Of course, it's all about the surface. I once asked the president of a leading PR firm which place in Asia was the most difficult to deal with. To my surprise, he replied 'Bangkok!' He launched into a diatribe: 'People in Bangkok are treacherous, two-faced, they'll steal your know-how and your clients, and you'll never realize what's going on until it's too late. I really hate trying to do business in Bangkok!'

In short, the grace is a reflective sheet of ice covering a deep black water. Underneath lies cunning and lots of unhappiness. If 'courtier' is the default mode of Thailand, then byzantine stratagems are also part of the paradigm.

As *farang* (Westerners), we miss the danger signs because we get the benefit of the hierarchy, which is what *marayaat* is all about. Thais tend to place *farang* in a higher role, and the *wais* get even nicer if you are also well off. Plus, in Western societies, we're simply not used to such indirectness. You need to listen carefully or you may not notice the subtle criticism aimed at you. There may be no criticism at all – until suddenly one day you are dropped.

Thais have spent their whole lives manoeuvring through the minefields of politeness. Westerners have not, and so we're woefully ill prepared to deal with the trouble when it comes. In the meantime we float blissfully in the rosy clouds of *marayaat* all around us.

Life is not so rosy for Thais lower on the scale, such as the poor, who suffer harsh scoldings from their bosses, or are preyed upon by low life in the slums. *Marayaat* is thus the producer of a Great Illusion, and the more privileged your position in society, the more you can get lost in it.

The expression one hears so often in Thailand *jai yenyen* ('keep a cool heart') exists for the very reason that Thais can be so hot-blooded. The calculus of rank and hierarchy means that human relations are rarely what they seem to be. You never can tell how much a gracious smile is due to simple good feeling, or maybe some other estimation is going on.

In society at large, censorship rules. In its gentler forms, censorship works through informal 'guidance' from state ministries; more scary is the danger of offending powerful people who might take revenge. Journalists and politicians also must watch their words for fear of being caught in the net of lèse majesté suits. Over time, everyone learns how to carefully self-censor, expressing ideas through innuendo and metaphor.

In order to read the newspapers, you have to learn the code: 'influential persons' may mean 'gangsters'; 'honest mistake' suggests that someone has been found guilty but is too powerful to be punished. Some topics are so sensitive that there are simply no allowable words for them. Thailand finds itself riven with deep problems that people can't talk about. Much is unexpressed; powerful emotions with volcanic power lie hidden below the censored surface.

Meanwhile, Bangkok is getting more globalized, and more middle-class. Proust pointed out that the nobility and the peasants share the same approach to life: they're bound to the land, and they value old places such as temples or churches. They respect social ranks, but at the same time they're free-spirited when it comes to sex, drink and so on. Ping's aristocratic family shared much in common with immigrants from the rice fields of the North and Northeast.

The middle class opposes both these groups. They care little for old places; they don't much value social ranks because, for them, it's the money that counts. On the other hand, they favour a prim and Victorian morality. This is the group that supports the closing of nightlife by 1 a.m., and a proposal in 2006 that the drinking age be raised to twenty-four. While strong on 'moral' issues like drinking, they are less concerned with the fine points of etiquette that people in old Thai society had to learn.

Anti-litter sign at Benchasiri Park by 'SMILE' (municipal campaign).

Meanwhile, the countryside is also changing. The migrants who bring their old-style values into the city are the last generation to grow up in wooden houses surrounded by water buffalo. In just ten years most of the villages of northern Thailand went from teak houses on stilts to concrete; where the villagers used to buy most necessities from their local market, now they go shopping at the giant Tesco Lotus store on the highway. The next generation of farmers will start out as 'middle-class' themselves.

The middle class will have the final victory in Bangkok. Their culture will be mall-culture. Street life and the free-and-easy attitudes that made the city so *sanuk* are already disappearing as we enter the 2020s. It's the unstoppable trend of history.

Millions of people in this new middle class lead lives of comfort and even luxury that could only be envied by their parents and the peoples of neighbouring countries who still remain poor. They're better informed, and linked to the world via the internet. They're politically savvy; hopes for Thai democracy rest on their shoulders. Their disdain for old-fashioned hierarchy is a form of freedom. They call their songs and fashion *inter* for 'international' and *indie* for 'independent'.

Yet even with these big changes, the instincts of politeness, instilled since childhood, survive. They even thrive in the middle class, as people try to act and look more genteel. Today *marayaat* is taught to children in schools with charts and diagrams. I think that all the shopping centres and Tesco Lotuses will hardly make a dent in the cult of politeness. It will take centuries to change this. The voices on the malls' PA systems, surrealistically soft and polite, whisper sugary encouragement to be nice.

Even polite Japan is no match for Thailand when it comes to gentleness. The politeness is there, but at critical moments Japan's fatal flaw, rigidity, spoils the effect. A flexible and ad hoc approach to life gives the Thais the wit and endurance to remain unfailingly pleasant, even in unhappy circumstances. It's a huge achievement, for there simply is no other country that manages it.

At the height of Covid-19 in 2020, the government health authorities produced a promotional video urging people not to share spoons when eating together, previously a common sight in Thai communal eating. In the video, a gaggle of gibbering virus zombies chases after terrified diners – until defeated by a man wielding his personal spoon. Surely no other country in the world responded to Covid-19 with anything this zany and hilarious. Whatever happens, a smile shines through.

Sensational novels teach us that Bangkok is a dangerous wild-east sort of place dominated by drugs, prostitution and an exotic underworld. For many Westerners, appalled at the bad air and bad traffic, it typifies the unsavoury Third World. Above all, the deep rift within society that leads now and then to upheavals such as the battles between the Red and Yellow Shirts is a sobering reality. As of 2021, we're still under military rule, which just barely keeps a lid on the pressure cooker.

Yet behind these problems, the broad river of 'Thai grace' flows steadily. Citizens of Bangkok speak and walk softly, smile as much as they can, move with natural grace, and fine-tune their interactions in order to cause others the least possible discomfort. From this point of view, one would have to call Bangkok the world's most civilized city.

Tiles and Flames 9
เส้นสายลายศิลป์

เขตงามวิจิตร

T he other day a Finnish and a Thai friend were visiting at my apartment, and as it got late, we ordered in pizza for dinner. With it came little packets of ketchup. The Finn and I dabbed a few blotches of ketchup here and there on our pizza slices. The Thai took pains to squeeze the ketchup out in narrow lines, crisscrossing from top to bottom of the slice.

That was *Lai Thai* at work. Meaning 'Thai patterns', *Lai Thai* are the design motifs that we see everywhere around us in Bangkok; they're what make the city look distinctively 'Thai'. Whenever you see a twisting *chofa* temple finial, or a heavenly maiden draped in golden ornaments (and we see a lot of those in Bangkok), you're viewing *Lai Thai*. So ingrained is *Lai Thai* in the fabric of Thai life that we don't usually stop to think about what these designs really are.

I first began to give some thought to *Lai Thai* when I opened my *benjarong* ceramics shop on Sukhumvit Road in 1998. After we had been selling *benjarong* for a while, I found that I was seeing this decoration everywhere. The same motifs cover the Grand Palace and Wat Pho, with their columns and *chedi* spires inlaid with shards of Chinese crockery and mirrored glass. Similar designs are embroidered on to the robes of masked Khon dancers.

The desire to cover every square inch with detail seems to have been there right at the start, as we can see from

Late-period Ban Chiang pot with swirl markings, *c.*300 BC.

Ban Chiang pottery from northeast Thailand, thought to be among the world's oldest. These pots have lines carved or drawn on the surface in a repeating pattern, sometimes squares and triangles, and other times fingerprint-like whorls.

The Ban Chiang Period was thousands of years ago, and nobody knows how the people of that time are related to the people who live in Thailand today. Nonetheless, those prehistoric patterns feel a lot like *Lai Thai* – the spirit of Siam's ancient inhabitants is still with us.

The shapes of *Lai Thai* that we see today trace to Thailand's neighbours in more recent eras. As they did with architecture and religion, the Thais borrowed.

The patterns carved on the lintels at Angkor Wat became the basis of *Lai Thai*. The Siamese court took the Angkorian motifs (which themselves had come from India via Java) and refined them. They added fine-grained detail, mixing in, at the final stage, flower and vine designs from China. Yet the curious thing about Thai forms is that, no matter where they originally came from, they can be instantly recognizable as Thai. I began to wonder what the secret is.

Tiles

In the process of studying *Lai Thai* in our course at the Origin Programme, it emerged that there are two types of *Lai Thai*. No one to my knowledge has yet defined these in English, so I've given them names: 'tiles' and 'flames'.

'Tiles' are designs inscribed within a square or circle, which fit together to cover a larger surface, like tiles on a wall. You can see the process at work in the buildup of the *prajam yam* design, a simplified version of which has been adopted as the Logo of Bangkok.

To draw a *prajam yam*, inscribe a circle inside a square, and then add four petals. Then indent and double the petals. Add extra rings to the circle. That's one 'tile', which could be square- or diamond-shaped. Link up a series of these, and you get a 'tiled' surface of *prajam yam* patterns, such as you might see on a *benjarong* plate.

From here, patterns can grow very elaborate. These are what we see on the columns of the Grand Palace and

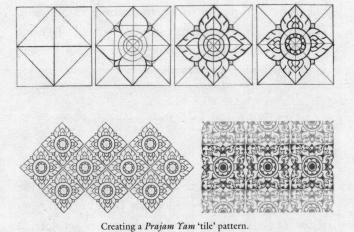

Creating a *Prajam Yam* 'tile' pattern.

154

Wat Po, shimmering with the pinks, yellows, blues and greens of shards of Chinese pottery which have been glued together to make up the 'tiles'.

Flames

'Flames' are what you find at the edges of things, wavy snake-like patterns that flare outwards, such as the swirling train of an angel's robe portrayed on a temple wall. The most striking prototype of this style is *chofa* finials, the curving wooden pieces that rise from the eaves of Thai temples and palaces.

As we learned in the Origin Programme, the primal shape, from which most Flame patterns are derived, is called *lai kranok*. It's the shape of the *kranok* leaf, which looks like a lopsided spade. After you've drawn one *kranok*, draw smaller *kranok* inside it, and even smaller *kranok* inside of them.

With that first step, you've gone inwards. In the next step, you take these *kranok* shapes and expand them outwards. You draw *kranok* shapes again and again– some

Creating a *lai kranok* 'flame' pattern.

Flame-like manes drawn with *lai kranok* pattern.

are drawn large, some small – and, as you go, you extend the tapered ends into a flickering branch. That's how to draw a *Lai Thai* 'flame'.

From here, the flames merge with human and animal forms, becoming the wings, tails and flaring manes that are so typical of Thai art.

As we practised drawing these patterns, it dawned on me that what is going on is 'fractal'.

'Fractal' is a term describing what happens when you start with a small set of rules and then repeat them, giving rise to systems of surprising complexity. In mathematics you start with '1+1=2', and a few rules about multiplying and dividing, and pretty soon you've generated all the chaotic infinitude of numbers.

Science has found that fractals are the key to the way things are shaped in nature, whether it's a quantum wave or river valley systems. All fractal patterns share a certain look, and it's exactly the look of Thai 'tiles', which link up

Fractals in nature: repetitive fractals in the shapes of lightning, snowflakes, corals, shells, ferns and cactus.

to cover a surface (fish scales, crystals, skin cells), and 'flames' which uncurl or branch outwards (ferns, shells, lightning). There's a reason why Thai patterns are so satisfying. They bear within them the seed of how the cosmos works.

Because they grow out of repetition, fractal patterns have the trait that, no matter at what scale you look at them, the patterns appear roughly the same. So tiny fibres in a corner of a leaf look like the veins of the whole leaf, and this pattern is in turn reflected in the spread of the twigs and branches of the whole tree.

157

The parts mimic the whole, and the whole reflects the parts. With *Lai Thai*, in the 'flame' design that looks like twisting fire or twirling tendrils, you can still see the basic *kranok* leaf at several levels of enlargement.

In exploring this fractal approach to line drawing over the centuries, the Siamese came up with many an ingenious technique, and in recent years these have been codified into books. Just as *marayaat* (etiquette) seems on the surface so free and easy but is decreed by rules that are taught in schools and published in books and posters, so is *Lai Thai*. There's a way to do things.

Next after line comes colour. Japan's paradigm colour is brown, the shade of aged temple columns, or a tea master's bland kimono. Unpainted wood, unglazed pottery – these things are part of *shibui*, 'low key', Japan's highest aesthetic. In Thailand, the concept of *shibui* is nearly unthinkable, except perhaps in old ruins. Thailand revels in a scintillating rainbow of colours. Temples and palaces, both inside and outside, sparkle with brilliant inlaid glass and gold arabesques.

The primary colour is gold. According to legend, a kingdom known as the Golden Land, or Suvarnabhumi, once ruled over the basin of the Chao Phraya River. Suvarnabhumi has since become the name of Bangkok International Airport. 'Golden Land' is appropriate, because one can hardly think of Thai art without seeing gold everywhere: golden pagodas, gold-leafed Buddhas and the golden outlines of *Lai Thai*.

The vivid colours likely have to do with the Thai love of *sanuk*, which inspired another key element of Thai design, namely 'transformation'. The eddying patterns of *Lai Thai* never stay put. One moment they are vines and leaves; then they look more like flames; these fuse into beaks, wings or claws; at the end they emerge as vines again.

Pageantry

The whole thrust of royal Siamese culture since Ayutthaya was the building of fantasy worlds, ethereal realms that are not of this earth. A lot of thought and choreography goes into creating illusion. When the King used to meet foreign ambassadors in the 1600s, he would wait until they all gathered; then a curtain would be pulled back, revealing him on a high golden throne, a vision of the divine.

Bangkok goes on doing gorgeous pageantry, especially at times of royal anniversaries, such as we experienced in 2007 (King Rama IX's eightieth birthday), and 2019 (the accession of King Rama X).

One form the pageantry takes is the *sum*, or decorative arches, which started in the early twentieth century. Perhaps the first was a royal celebration arch in the form of elephants with raised trunks spanning Ratchadamnoen Avenue, built in 1907 in honour of King Rama V's return from a trip to Europe. It's believed that the King was inspired by the arches he saw in Europe.

In recent years *sum* arches have boomed, spurred by

159

Sum chalerm prakiert: ceremonial arch over Ratchadamnoen Nok
Avenue in honour of King Rama IX's eightieth birthday.

the growing role of the monarchy in official life. Some
towns such as Chiang Mai boast *sum khao mueang*
('entering-town *sum*') spanning the roads at the city's
edge. In Bangkok the most dramatic *sum* still arch over
Ratchadamnoen, the royal avenue leading from the
Sanam Luang parade grounds eastwards to the Golden
Mount.

Those in charge of commissioning *sum* expend much
effort in their design. You see *sum* piled up with layers
of angels, lotus buds, elephants and clouds, painted in
gold, pink and purple with swirling *Lai Thai* motifs.

Grand *sum* flourish in the old part of town, with its
concentration of palaces and government offices. In
fact, most romantic architecture is found here. The rest
of the city tends definitely to the drab, which has got
Bangkok its reputation as disordered and ugly. But even
in the modern sectors, you encounter variants of *sum*.

One of the first things that visitors see after arrival at Suvarnabhumi International Airport is a big *sum* over the expressway.

In addition to the *sum*, throughout town are golden *krueang ratchasakkara*, royal altars, honouring royal family members. Some of these tower three metres or more; smaller versions stand at the entrances to banks and office buildings and at street corners.

Amidst Bangkok's clutter, glamour expresses itself in *sum* arches and *krueang ratchasakkara* altars. We see these things so often that it's easy to dismiss them as trite public displays of 'Thainess'. But from the point of view of the creativity that goes into them, they are truly

Krueang ratchasakkara: decorative altar honouring
King Rama IX and Queen Sirikit.

epiphanies of decorative art. I can't think of another big city with anything like this.

Efflorescence

Although different on the surface, Japan and Thailand share many similarities, one of which is: they're both copycats. China and India were 'primal' places where religion and the basic forms of Asian civilization were born. Japan and Thailand, on the other hand, can hardly claim a single thing in their traditional cultures that didn't come from somewhere else.

Look closely at anything Japanese, even something as ancient and local as Shinto religion, and you find Daoism in disguise. In Thailand, likewise, architecture came from Angkor, Buddhism from Sri Lanka, lower dress from India, upper dress from China. And yet both countries transformed those foreign influences to the extent that Japanese things look immediately and distinctively 'Japanese', and the same is true for Thailand.

If one were to describe the difference, it would be that the Japanese approach is to refine and strip away the non-essential, whereas in Thailand it's just the opposite. Japan abstracts; Thailand effloresces. The Japanese took Chinese temples, did away with green glazed tiles and red lacquer, reducing roofs to grey-black and columns to unpainted brown wood. The Thais took Khmer motifs from Angkor, repeated them at large and small scales until they grew into the extravagant curlicues of *Lai Thai* – and then covered all that with glitter.

For Japan, the fact that so little originated there has been a source of mortification, and there's a huge literature devoted to proving that Japan is 'unique'. Thailand seems less troubled by this, and it might be the result of having always been a busy crossroads, rather than an island.

Despite the similarities in their cultural history, when it comes to design, Thailand and Japan are truly opposites. Japanese art focuses Zen-like on the moment, on the matter at hand. The emphasis is on purity, on isolating each entity and savouring it for what it is.

In Thailand, everything gets mixed up, fish are strung together like flowers, temple bases flare out like flower petals, *chofa* finials could be birds' beaks or elephant trunks. Nothing ends up the way it started out.

While their methods may differ, for both countries it's all about creating a beautiful surface. Japan and Thailand share the fact that both countries value surface over content, and this also applies to the calm and pleasantry of society. As long as everyone keeps properly bowing and *wai*-ing, injustices and misery disappear from view. While neither country is more just or gentle than its neighbours – in some ways, they can be harsher – they feel like happy places because the surface mood of daily life is so 'user-friendly'.

Beguiled by deferential bows, foreign visitors easily fall into a utopian illusion about Japan and Thailand, whereas robust modern China never allows you to relax for a minute. Few imagine utopia there. But in Thailand or Japan, it's easy to float away on the pleasant surface. These countries are 'Lotus Lands', where the visitor drinks the magical lotus wine that makes him forget his former life, and indeed forget about the basics of human nature. Such as the fact that common sense tells us: there must be more behind that Thai smile.

The Beguiling Surface

In the sphere of art, the surface details of *Lai Thai* came over time to so predominate over 'form' that they became form itself. The Buddha dissolves into the golden filigree that encrusts and enthrones him.

All this baroque glitz runs directly against our modern point of view. In the West we spent the twentieth century stripping away the ostentatious frippery of earlier centuries, and today we value pure and abstract forms above all. Japan was ideally suited to be 'modern' because the default mode for Japanese shapes was simple and abstract. Thailand falls at the opposite end of the scale.

In the West, therefore, Thai art has been seen as 'decorative' and has never achieved high prices in the global art market. Western museums and private collectors vie for Khmer art and will happily spend millions of dollars for a fine Angkorian sculpture. It's because of the simple and noble strength of those Khmer torsos. But I can hardly think of a major museum that has specialized in Thai. If they have a good piece, it's because an eccentric collector like Doris Duke left it to them. Thai art is just not seen as important, and Thai culture has thus had little impact on the world.

There are 'important' countries and unimportant countries. Americans know all too well that we're important, and so do the British, French, Chinese and Japanese. But what about the Poles or the Finns? In Japan, we take for granted that tea ceremony and so forth will be taken seriously by the world. Not here. Thailand – for scholars in prestigious universities, for the nabobs of culture in New York and Paris – is an insignificant place, a tourist curiosity.

The arts we study at the Origin Programme in Bangkok are not those that have influenced, or probably ever will influence, the globe. The world sees Thailand's culture as 'minor' – it's one of those things one must accept when you are living in Bangkok. That's fine by me. For those of us who have come to love Thai arts, we feel we've found a jewel that everyone else overlooked.

It's back to 'Thai grace', which we first encountered in *marayaat* etiquette. The process of 'grace-ifying' has been going on for centuries. Tribal taboos, such as that against raising a roof towards the sky, as explained by John Blofeld, were refined and refined until they reached the inexpressible elegance of the *chofa* roof finials.

The fingers of sculpted Buddhas stretched, and their eyelids curved; headdresses rose like pagoda spires and wavered like flames; the right-angle disappeared; *Lai*

Thai twisted and flowered until it reached fractal dimensions. The Thais took their ancient sense of man and universe and polished the surface until they raised the surface itself to the plane of heaven.

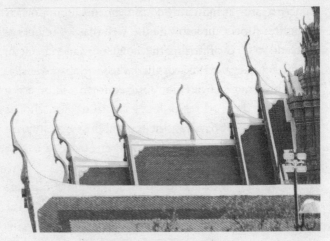

Chofa finials at the Grand Palace.

Contemporary Thai artists have not been able to escape *Lai Thai*'s power. Even in the modern paintings that flank the corridors and luggage belts at the airport you'll find liberal use of *Lai Thai*. Yet for contemporary artists *Lai Thai* is as much a burden as a blessing. The frills and gilded frou-frous don't lend themselves well to conceptual art, which dominates on the global scene.

I've had an ongoing argument for some years with an Australian museum director about the merits of

Thailand's great artist Thawan Duchanee, who died in 2014. For me, Thawan was a genius, a modern master of fractal line. Into that line he brought raw, powerful emotions. I believe that a century from now, Thawan will be revered for his images that combine *Lai Thai* vividly, sometimes shockingly, with eagles, horses, human body parts. But for my director friend, Thawan was just more Thai kitsch. He preferred the conceptual approach of Montien Boonma (1953–2000), whose abstract installations broke away from the Thai concern with surface finesse.

Modern artists have only begun to explore the expressive richness hidden within *Lai Thai*. They stand in a position similar to the Chinese and Japanese artists who tried to modernize calligraphy. It didn't look up-to-date or Western enough to please modern art experts, to the extent that one Japanese critic in the late nineteenth century commented, 'Calligraphy is not an art.' Only in the

Digital numbers / universes in modern *Lai Thai* by
Thongchai Srisukprasert: (*left*) 'Zero'; (*right*) 'One'.

late twentieth century did a new breed of calligraphers appear who rediscovered the power of the brush and gained international renown.

Lai Thai, like calligraphy, is pure line, and only in the last few decades have artists started to explore what a contemporary approach might be to its fractal qualities. In the paintings of one of the pioneers, Thongchai Srisukprasert, the flaring lines of *Lai Thai* flames explode into electrically charged dynamos and expanding galaxies.

I remember as a student coming to Bangkok for the first time and being haunted by the ins and outs, the unexpected twists and turns, of the *chofa* rising from temple eaves. The words to describe that quality go beyond mere decorative appeal. They would be: 'mastery of line' and 'the power of cosmic fractals'.

In any case, trying to be minimal and conceptual misses the point. They can do that in New York or Tokyo just as well, or usually much better. Nobody in the world (not even Thailand's neighbours, Cambodia and Myanmar) can begin to accomplish the ethereal miracle of *Lai Thai*. The flickering flames of *Lai Thai* are Thailand's great contribution to world art.

The struggle between the two camps of the Internationalists epitomized by Montien and the *Lai Thai* drawers led by Thawan and Thongchai will only intensify as Thailand's artists try to break into the world art market. But we can leave those issues to the curators and galleries. For me, living surrounded by *Lai Thai* motifs is one of the pleasures of Bangkok, just as seeing calligraphy everywhere is part of the fun of Hong Kong or Tokyo. So specific are these patterns that one glance at just a fragment of *Lai Thai* is enough to tell you, 'This is Thai.'

Saeb
เลิศรสสะกดใจ

เขตสยิวชิวหา

10

What follows is the record of a conversation about Thai food that took place one night at my apartment. The cast of characters was:

Vithi Phanichphant, professor at Chiang Mai University

Dr Navamintr 'Taw' Vitayakul, owner of Ruen Urai restaurant

Num, my neighbour

Saa, my assistant

171

Cameron 'Cam' McMillan, guest from New Zealand

Vithi: When you boil it down to essentials, there are three things that make up Thai food: curry from India, coconut and jungle flavours from the Mon, and Chinese stir-fry. It's a mix, a variety. You could call it the primitive taste, the curry taste and the stir-fried taste, and often they overlap. For example, Chinese-based food can have spiciness, curry can have the consistency of Chinese watery soup (instead of thick as in India), and curry also might have lemongrass (the jungly taste).

Num: It's like having sex with every part of your body at the same time.

Vithi: There's no monotony. It delivers a variety of senses to the taste buds, so all your taste buds are stimulated at the same time.

Alex: I guess this is why you can hardly find a city anywhere in the world without a Thai restaurant.

Vithi: Zesty. *Saeb*. That's an Isarn word similar to the Thai *aroi* (delicious). While *aroi* signifies in general something pleasant to eat, *saeb* has oomph. It makes you sweat.

Alex: Would you say that Thai food ranks as a world cuisine?

Taw: Yes. We were one of the first to fuse, before people knew about fusion food. Can you think of any food in the world that gives you so many flavours in one mouthful? Taste – sweet, salty, sour, slightly bitter, sometimes spicy, slightly oily. Texture – sometimes crispy and soft in one mouthful. Temperature – hot and cold.

Think of the hot, crispy catfish fried rice overlaid with strips of cold, stringent green mango we're eating now. That's so typically Thai. Some people use the word 'primordial' to describe Thai food; it comes direct to your senses. Flavour, texture and temperature, all combined in one go. Vietnamese comes close but lacks a certain zing. Thai explodes in the mouth.

Then there's the matter of regional cooking. Thai food is like Chinese or French or Italian – with many regional cuisines and variations. There's the food from the four regions, the Northeast, North, Central and South. We mix it all together in one meal.

Fusion

Cam: Where did the fusion take place?

Num: It happened in Bangkok, the capital.

Taw: I think it started long before Bangkok. For thousands of years we've been living in this piece of land sandwiched between China, India and the southern islands. We take the best out of everything and use it.

The Northeast is influenced by Lao and Khmer, concentrating on fresh grilled things. The Khmers focus on salad, or something fresh. The Isarn approach is *som tam* (papaya salad with tomato, dried crabs or shrimps, and crushed garlic or chilli). It's salad, grilled food, steamed things.

Vithi: Be careful of what you call 'Isarn'. *Som tam* came from America. Look at all the ingredients: we never had most of them. Papaya, tomato and *phrik* (chillies) – they all came from the New World.

Taw: Yes, *som tam* is questionable. And *pad thai* (fried flat noodles with dried shrimps, peanuts, bean sprouts and egg), even though it uses the word 'Thai' in its name, is really Chinese, although some say Vietnamese.

Vithi: The only thing that's truly Isarn is *plaa raa* (fermented fish).

Alex: How did they put it all together?

Making *som tam* salad in a mortar.

Vithi: In the case of *som tam*, they had the concept of it long before. They had the *som*, which means 'sour' – it meant sour fruits such as mango, star apple and Thai olives. *Tam* means 'crushed'. All of these were crushed in a small mortar and mixed to make the original salads. They got replaced by American ingredients.

Taw: Another aspect of the fusion is that we took food from all over Southeast Asia, going as far as Muslim food also.

Alex: I've read that King Narai in the mid seventeenth century loved Persian food.

Taw: We fused everything. We fused the dishes, the style of cooking, and we fused the ingredients. We got egg desserts from Portugal. Of course you know the New World ingredients, which came via Portugal and India: potato, chillies, tomatoes, papayas, corn, peanuts.

Vithi: We never had anything like that. The only thing we knew was mango and coconut.

Num: We didn't eat anything, that's why we were so skinny before. Fusion made us obese!

Taw: Now there are even newer things available. We have salmon, but when we prepare it at my restaurant, it becomes salmon in *jaeo* (powdered chilli sauce with lime). That makes it Thai food; it's made with new ingredients.

Num: It's Thai food gone *inter* and *indie*.

Taw: One of the basic flavours of Thai food is *nam phrik* (chilli paste).

Vithi: But just imagine, we didn't have the *phrik* chillies before, either! That too came from the New

175

World. The oldest taste is *nam plaa*, the fish sauce – the very distinctive ingredient of Thai food is *nam plaa*.

Alex: Like soy sauce in Japan. Everything Japanese has soy sauce in it somewhere.

Taw: That's the basic thing. You boil something, and it becomes like a *tom yam* soup. Boil it more, add some Indian influence, with fresh herbs and coconut milk, and it becomes a *kaeng* soup of some kind. Without the curry paste you have *kaeng lueang* (peppery mixed vegetable soup) or *kaeng som* (sour soup made of tamarind paste). That's quite Thai.

Cam: Why would you call the sour *kaeng som* soup 'quite Thai'?

Taw: It's sour, it's spicy. It's an odd combination: sour and spicy. Then you have fried food. Anything that's done in a wok is Chinese: fried, stir-fried, sautéed, all Chinese. And then you have Muslim food, such as potato in so-called massaman curry.

Saa: But it's strange, the potato comes from America. I wonder what would happen if we hadn't found America?

Num: Alex wouldn't be here.

Vithi: You have to realize that we didn't eat this way before. This kind of texture of a clear soup [*kaeng jeud*] was new to us. We didn't have clear soup, which is basically from China.

Cam: Speaking of soup, why is it that they never serve the soup with little bowls to serve yourself?

Num: Because it's a shared thing.

Saa: Thais don't like to divide things up. At my family, there is only one large soup bowl, and everybody eats together.

Vithi: I call the people of Lanna and the Mekhong area the 'sticky rice people'. The sticky rice people *jim nam*, that is, they *jim* (dip) into *nam* (water), but that refers to anything watery. They didn't use a spoon to scoop. Roll up the ball of sticky rice, stick it into the soup. Eat the juice first, and then the vegetables and meat comes later. They don't really have spoons.

Num: It's like a little sponge.

Spoons and New Ideas

Alex: You say that the Thais traditionally didn't have spoons. But they certainly do now. It was one of the big differences I noticed when I started coming here from Japan: Thais rarely use chopsticks; they eat with spoons and forks. When did these come in?

Vithi: It was King Rama VI in the 1920s. He brought it back from public school in England. We have changed our way of eating so much. That's why *khanom jiin* (fresh rice noodles with saucy curry, vegetables and pickles) became popular.

Alex: They say *khanom jiin* is the food of the Mon people, who were here long before the Thai tribes arrived. What really is the core Mon food?

177

Vithi: Anything with coconut is Mon.

Saa: Who was coming up with these ideas?

Vithi: Basically these early fusions are court food. The Mon who made the fusions were ladies at the court in Bangkok. All these court ladies, they had nothing to do, they had leftovers from this and that, and they made them into nice things. They had some leftover vegetables, leftover shrimp paste, leftover red onions, anything left over they would think up ways to use it to make something unusual. The royal people would say, 'Oh, this looks good, we'll have it.' But actually it was just leftovers. The palace adopted what was originally Mon cuisine and then elaborated it into more varieties, and then they beautified by adding carved vegetables in the form of flowers. Thai food is basically a mix between Chinese and Mon.

Alex: Thai culture in general seems to have resulted from a collision between Chinese and Mon.

Vithi: In Mon food, the raw taste is always there.

Alex: Whereas Indian and Chinese food are usually very cooked, not many simple or raw flavours.

Cam: For me, Chinese food is what really boring Thai food would taste like.

Taw: Thai process and technique are not as sophisticated as the French, but it's about creative use of ingredients. Substitution. If the right vegetable isn't available, use another. We're not too strict about using a particular ingredient. If we can't find unripened papaya, then we'll use unripened mango. That's how the fusion started.

Alex: It's such a difference from Japanese food, where the emphasis is on perfect ingredients. Chefs make sure that a particular leaf of the season arrives at just the right time. That so impressed the Michelin Guide people, to the extent that they gave Tokyo more gold stars even than Paris. Which upset a lot of people in France. I don't think Michelin would appreciate the Thai easy-going approach.

Taw: Some things can be substituted. If the fish or vegetable is not in season, find something that is. On the other hand, there are certain things that you can never substitute. For example, fish cakes or fish balls made from *plaa krai* fish. The consistency, the gluey texture is perfect for certain dishes, and nothing else will do. Generally speaking, meats are variable. You can have a green curry with chicken, beef, pork or fish, and it doesn't matter. But spices and herbs are important. You've got to get these right.

Alex: On the subject of spices, my cousin Tom points out that the Thai dinner table always has three or four condiments. People flavour their food as they like, to make it sweeter (sugar), saltier (fish sauce), more sour (vinegar) or hotter (chilli powder). He relates this to the easy-going give-and-take of Thai society. Everyone is allowed to be what they are and do more or less what they want.

Vithi: If you think of a typical Thai meal that most of the population would prefer to have: you have a *kaeng* of some kind (curry, a watery thing); a bowl of chilli paste and a vegetable – something raw and fresh, like salad; and then you have a *phad* (something stir-fried), a *neung* (steamed thing), a *thawt* (deep fried), or *yaang* (grilled), or even a light soup, which is very Chinese. So you have primitive food, the Indian style and the Chinese style. Those are the three.

Alex: It seems that almost everything the Thais eat today is new in some way. Things that I thought went very far back turn out to be recent creations, thought up in the nineteenth or even mid-twentieth century.

Cam: You've all left one thing out. What about the grasshoppers, ants' eggs, and so on that you see Thais eating?

Vithi: Insects are really old, part of the original menu. It goes back before human beings were 'hunters and gatherers', to when we were just 'gatherers', living on berries and roots and insects in the forest.

Cam: Yes, but most developed societies in the world stopped eating insects long ago. Why do they continue in Thailand?

Vithi: Because they're so good! Delicious and crunchy. Think of the tangy flavour of juice from the *maengda* waterbeetle.

Num: It tastes a little like apricot essence.

Vithi: Plus, bugs are a source of protein.

Alex: I guess I should amend what I said about the new-ness of Thai food. Some really ancient things survive here when they've died out elsewhere.

Vithi: It's the same with *baisri* flower arrangements. It's something very old.

Alex: Yes, but *baisri* are something you see at rituals, not every day. Did people ever actually decorate their homes with flowers?

Taw: We have potted plants.

Vithi: That's Chinese bonsai.

Cam: You mean the potted plants aren't Thai?

Taw: In Thai houses, there isn't much to decorate. There's hardly any furniture, a few chairs or tables, or sometimes nothing. Maybe a *tang* (low table).

Vithi: *Tang*, too, is Chinese. If you're a scholar, you had a *tang* to write on.

Alex: So we're fusing Chinese furniture and bonsai with the interior of Southeast Asian houses.

Num: Siam is the crossroads of everything.

Taw: Even patterns. You have patterns originally from India or China that go to Angkor in Cambodia first, and then come to us.

Vithi: Everything is inherited from Angkor. Most of what makes up classical culture in Bangkok, that is. Someone once said, 'Bangkok is the last gasp, the last breath of Angkor.'

Taw: The classic form for traditional *Lai Thai* design is the Khmer *kranok*, and it's been modified into many different forms.

Thep phanom: praying angel arising from vines.

Alex: *Kranok* looks like a sort of lopsided tear shape. What does it derive from?

Saa: Some say it comes from a lotus bud, some say jasmine flowers, some say from the little leaf-buds that sprout at the joints of bamboo or sugar cane.

Taw: It's not just a matter of what's drawn or painted. You have things that are three-dimensional, like petals on architectural bases, things that become architectural elements.

Vithi: Those petals at the feet of columns, they're protective petals.

Num: Columns fusing with flowers now.

Vithi: Actually, think of *thep phanom*, the decorative motif you see all over Bangkok. It's the upper torso of an angel, hands clasped in prayer, but the lower body is vines and leaves. A fusion between angel and vegetable.

Num: Sounds delicious. Are we still talking about food here?

The Elephant-Bird

Vithi: The ultimate fusion motif is the *chofa* finials of Thai temples. They are derived from the divine elephant-bird, *nok hatsadiling*.

Taw: I thought the *chofa* of Thailand came from winged Garuda.

Himmaphan creatures transform into architecture:
(*left*) *nok hatsidiling*, combining elephant, bird and snake;
(*right*) *chofa* finial derived from *nok hatsidiling*.

183

Vithi: Not Garuda. It's a triple combination of bird plus elephant plus *nak* (serpent). They call this elephant-bird *hatsidiling*. Temples are believed to be standing in the foothills of Mount Meru, and in these foothills is the sacred forest *Himmaphan*, full of legendary mixed-up animals. The elephant-bird is one of the creatures of *Himmaphan*.

Alex: You can see statues of some of those creatures in the grounds of the Grand Palace: angels in the form of half-lion/half-man and half-lion/half-woman. Or a bird with the upper body of a *yak* (demon).

Vithi: *Nok hatsadiling*, the elephant-bird, has the curl of the elephant's trunk, has the beak and wings of the parrot and then the tail of the *nak* serpent. It's the representation of three states of animal: earth-bound, water-bound and air-bound.

Num: Like the Chakri Maha Prasat Throne Hall in the Grand Palace, which has neo-French Renaissance style marble columns and staircases down below, but Thai roofs at the top. It was called at the time, 'a *farang* wearing a Thai hat'. A European building with *chadaa* (Thai-style crowns) on top – that's quite a combination.

Vithi: There were various ways of adapting a foreign import to Thai style. One way is simply to stretch it out. Like the elongated *prang* (Angkor-style tower) such as you can see at Wat Arun in Bangkok. We took the *prang* from Angkor and elongated it to look more like a *chedi* (Thai-style stupa with a tall pointed spire).

Phra Thinang Chakri Maha Prasat Throne Hall: built in 1882, the neo-French
Renaissance body is topped by Thai-style crowns.

Alex: They took the Khmer artichoke and stretched it
into a Thai corn cob.

Vithi: The Khmer *prang* towers were Shiva linga. We
stretched out the Shiva lingam.

Alex: Made it longer and thinner.

Vithi: And added texture. Covered the whole surface
with shards of broken dishes.

Num: Ouch!

Alex: When it comes to language, I have this feeling that
any word with a *kra* or *pra* sound in it is going to be
Khmer in origin. It's common enough that languages
have a classical base from somewhere else. Where
would we be in English if we only had four-letter
Anglo-Saxon words and no Greek or Latin additions
like 'philosophy' or 'circumambulate'? If you look at

Korean and Japanese, they're filled with Chinese borrowings. But here, most of the foreign borrowings seem to be Khmer, Sanskrit and Pali.

Vithi: And Chinese, too. I think you can find plenty of Chinese words.

Alex: Obviously the numbers are from China. But I was disappointed. I came here thinking I could use more of my Chinese. I thought there would be more cognates. But there are very few, so in learning Thai I had to really start at zero.

Vithi: The words might not come from China, but the accent in Bangkok does. The official Thai language of Bangkok, the Bangkok pronunciation – it's Thai language with *Taechiu* accent.

Cam: Who are the *Taechiu*?

Vithi: A group of Chinese settlers who came from Chaozhou, a town in the eastern part of Guangzhou. They make up a big part of the Chinese community in Bangkok.

Alex: Actually we haven't talked much about the role of the Chinese in the Bangkok fusion, aside from cooking. But you can see Chinese touches everywhere. For example, in clothing. Like the 'fisherman's pants' Khun Taw is wearing.

Cam: I think of those as totally Thai. In fact, I thought they were called 'Thai pants'. What's Chinese about them?

Vithi: The name for them is *kangkeng* (trousers) plus *talay* or *lay* (sea). It was the Chinese who brought the notion of loose long trousers. Before that the Thai, at least the men, had only loincloths. As for the *talay*, 'the sea', it's because the Chinese arrived by sea. Nothing to do with fishermen.

Jongkrabane with Mutton Sleeves

Saa: What about women's dress?

Vithi: The ladies, the women of the court, wore *jong-krabane* (pantaloons consisting of one long cloth wound around the waist, and then pulled between the thighs and tied at the back). The *jongkrabane*, with roots in India, was the classic costume of Angkor, and the people of the court were inclined to Angkor style. Before the founding of Bangkok, in Ayutthaya they wore the more Thai-style *phasin* (straight-hanging sarong), but when the court moved to Bangkok, there was a vogue for things Khmer. It felt more classical.

Alex: Like the Romans trying to act like Greeks.

Vithi: They cut their hair short like the Khmer, and wore *jongkrabane* like Khmer. Then in the late nineteenth century came the Victorian influence. The short hair started to grow a little bit, to look like a lotus bud. At that time, this was the height of fashion. Not quite the beehive hairdo '*khunying* look' we're familiar with in Bangkok today.

Cam: What's *khunying*?

Alex: It's an honorary title, like the British 'Dame'. *Khunying* are wealthy, powerful women, and their

Windswept hair: the short hair of court ladies began to grow longer into a lotus bud shape.

hairstyle tends towards 'power hair'. Great masses of hair brushed back into a beehive or egg shape.

Vithi: At the end of the 1800s, the women of Paris had been inspired by the Japanese. 'Geisha hair' swept all before it. It was the love for things Oriental, so they had hair bundled on top, geisha-style. Back in Bangkok, they were trying to emulate Europe, but these ladies of the court, they had very short hair and couldn't manage the full geisha effect. So they put oil or wax and just combed their hair up like that, so it was like a small wave of hair, windblown, windswept. They had the mutton sleeves of a typical Victorian blouse, combined with the *jongkrabane*, and below that, stockings and the shoes.

| 1880s princess: European mutton sleeves, fan, *jongkrabane* and white stockings. | 1920s Gatsby – male: *rajapataen* jacket, *jongkrabane* and hat worn at a jaunty angle. | 1920s Gatsby – female: headband, flapper-style blouse, Thai *phasin* skirt and high heels. |

Taw: Mutton sleeves with *jongkrabane*.

Vithi: This is how fashion went: in the early period, it was the Western top and the Thai *jongkrabane* at the bottom.

Num: In the case of the Throne Hall, the top is Thai, and the bottom is *farang*. But for people, the top was *farang*, and the bottom was Thai.

Vithi: That was the Rama V look in the later nineteenth century.

Taw: But during King Rama VI's reign in the 1910s and 1920s, they switched from *jongkrabane* back to old-style Thai *phasin* textiles for their lower garment. But shorter than the old ones had been.

Vithi: The fashion for that period was 'Gatsby'. Rama VI tried to be a little bit nationalist, so let's wear the *phasin* (sarong), because it felt more 'Thai' than the Khmer *jongkrabane*. While the *phasin* used to come down to the ankles, now it came up and showed off the stocking and the shoes.

Rama VI's ladies had hair done in waves and had ribbons going around. It was the full Gatsby look, very flat, everything sleek and vertical; the *phasin* going down straight, and with high-heeled shoes.

Taw: It goes on like that for a while, but from the Second World War onwards, after Rama VIII, it's full-on Western.

Alex: But then there is a new development, post 1970s, when Queen Sirikit worked to revive traditional textiles such as *madmii* (ikat weave). She hired Parisian designers to design dresses for her using Thai fabrics, and she made it de rigueur for society ladies to wear those textiles. So now the emphasis is on Western styles, but using Thai weaving. It didn't end up as completely Western after all.

After this, we talked about other Thai-*farang* mixtures such as the *rajapataen* (official uniform for civil servants) for men, a starched white jacket with high collar, often combined with the *jongkrabane*. You see it at official functions, or worn by page boys in traditional hotels such as the Oriental. *Rajapataen* is the Thai pronunciation of 'Raja pattern', but it's not Indian; it's Russian. It appeared after Rama V went to visit Czar Nicolas at the Russian court in Saint Petersburg.

After *rajapataen*, we rather lost the thread of thought. As usual, when people start talking about Thailand, it ends up a muddle. Bangkok is like a *thep phanom*, a

Rajapataen: royal pages, *c.*1920, wearing *rajapataen* jackets and *jongkrabane*.

smiling angel with hands clasped in prayer above – and twirling vines and leaves below.

One word that kept coming up was 'fusion'. Right at the beginning of my Thai adventure, when I was spending time in the 1970s with the British-educated Svastis, I was dealing with one aspect of that fusion, which is between peoples. The big fusion, the one between the native Mon-Khmers and the Thai-Chinese, goes on and on. But there's also a fusion with the West and, in some cases, Westerners. Bangkok is full of mixed-blood Western-Thai children and their families.

Fusion is, of course, not unique to Thailand. Every civilization on earth has absorbed influences from else-where, even the great mother cultures of China and

India. However, in China and India (despite two centuries of British colonization on the subcontinent), the foreign influences tend to dissolve into the bigger soup of the original culture.

In Thailand, in contrast, you can still see and taste the original ingredients, as in Thai food: sweet, salty, sour, bitter, crispy and soft – all in one mouthful. Or like Bangkok's Grand Palace: Khmer, Javanese, Lao, Lanna, Thai, Chinese, Indian, Sri Lankan and European, all in one view.

Japan, despite its ready adaptation of foreign things, remains resolutely Japanese. It's part of the strength of the culture, because the Japanese have carefully preserved their core traditions. Think of the many changes that Thai women's dress has gone through, from *phasin* (native Thai sarongs), to *jongkrabane* (Khmer-style pantaloons) with Victorian 'mutton-sleeves', and finally *madmi* silks sewn into Western fashion. The kimono, during all this time, remained remarkably stable. The sense of purity that results has much appeal to foreigners and Japanese alike. In Japan, it's easier to get to the roots of things.

Yet, for all the great achievements of Japanese culture, one quality it cannot lay claim to is *saeb*, the word that Vithi used, the Isarn word for 'delicious'. It comes from lack of purity, from substitution, invention and play – all those *sanuk* things that make up the Thai fusion. Delicious plus zing.

Flowers

บุษบาบัณ

11

เขตปากคลองตลาด

T he whole world knows of Japanese *ikebana* and Chinese bonsai, but it comes as a surprise to many people that Thailand has its own flower tradition. People live here for years and never notice it.

Flowers had long been an interest of mine in Japan, and I was a bit disappointed when I began revisiting Bangkok again after 1989. Thais didn't decorate their homes with flowers in vases, as I was used to in Japan. Flower decor in public spaces, like hotels, tended to be masses of things stuffed in a jar in the style of Western

Baisri flower offering.

floral bouquets, or they mimicked the 'Balinese spa look', with petals strewn in basins of water and scattered over bed covers. There seemed nothing very Thai about flower arrangements in Thailand.

Then, in 1990, I made the first visit to a village in the northern province of Phayao. As a ceremony of welcome, the villagers prepared for us a *baisri* flower offering. Women and children gathered round, cutting and folding banana leaves into intricate patterns which they linked together into a structure – a sort of tower with wings or claws on the side. Along the edges of the wings they pinned tiny white flowers and surmounted the tower, which was about 30 centimetres high, with an egg and a spire of more little flowers. The village elder intoned prayers, and at the end of the ceremony all the villagers tied sacred threads around our wrists.

That was the first time that I witnessed Thai flowers in action. Still, I saw the *baisri* as a charming up-country custom, not as something important to Bangkok as well. The turning point came almost a decade later, when I made my first experiments in creating a Thai arts programme for a group of Japanese architects in 1998. Suan Pakkard Palace offered me their grounds to use for a one-day programme, and, based on what I was familiar with from Japan, I also included flowers.

The problem was: what would these 'flowers' consist of? I already had my doubts about Siamese gardens. As far as I could see, these mainly consisted of bonsai-like plantings looking like Western topiary, with everything trimmed to look like an ostrich or an elephant.

Nunie, my unofficial 'Thai auntie' with whom I spent so much time in the 1970s, was the aunt of my friend Ping. I asked Nunie to give the Japanese group a tour of the Suan Pakkard grounds, and as she did she pointed out how this tree was known for its scent, the one over there because it appeared in a classical poem; while other plants were valued as herbs that could be used for cooking. That said, I couldn't quite see what was Thai about the layout of the garden, since it basically consisted of a few trees surrounding a lawn of British-style mown grass.

Flowers as Geometry

For the grand finale of the Suan Pakkard programme, I engaged Paothong Thongchua to cater for the dinner. Paothong is one of the colourful figures of Bangkok's cultural renaissance of the late 1990s and early 2000s. A professor at Thammasat University, he's a scholar of textiles, an impresario of cultural events and owner of a string of antique shops and boutiques.

Paothong's dinner, served on the lawn of Suan Pakkard Palace, was the surprise event of the day. Each plate came accompanied by rings of banana leaves, layered and folded like the *baisri* I'd seen up north. The dinner display featured a variety of garlands and several *baisri* for the dance performance that concluded the evening. These *baisri*, some of them 50 centimetres or more in height, were far more complicated than those I had come across before. So intricate were Paothong's floral creations that I took home some of the 'plate ruffs' and pressed and dried them. I have them to this day.

What I realized at that dinner was that I had been looking in the wrong place for Thai flowers. I thought they would look like flowers.

In Japan, each arrangement is a portrait of the natural world. But flowers in Thailand leave nature far behind. Petals and leaves are raw materials, fragments of a fantasy architecture, like Lego pieces. They're cut and sliced, flattened, creased, sewn together by threads, attached by bamboo pins and then built up, piece by folded piece, into towers and wings. Flowers here are geometry.

After that first Origin event, I changed the focus of the flower component of the programme away from flowers as I had known them in Japan and China, that is, stems put in a vase. Those concepts were irrelevant in Thailand. I asked some teachers to come over and show us how they create the *baisri*.

What emerged as we practised making them in the Origin Programme was that the basic structure of the *baisri* is a *krathong*. The word means a 'leaf vessel' and it refers to a bowl or container made from folded and cut leaves (usually banana leaves).

Krathong can be as small as a 4-centimetre-square container for a Thai sweet. Or they can be giant extravaganzas of leaves folded into pin-wheels and sunflower shapes, embellished with carved fruit and threaded flowers, a metre or more in height. I now saw that the folded leaves surrounding Paothong's plates at the Suan Pakkard dinner event were a form of *krathong*.

The *krathong* is a quintessentially Southeast Asian

Basic *krathong*: *krathong* made from folded banana leaf.

Krathong built up into complex structure.

object, found everywhere from Thailand south to Indonesia. In Bali, you see local versions of *krathong*, little trays made from coconut leaves containing a few blossoms or petals, set out every morning as offerings along the roadside.

The *krathong* seem to have grown from living in the southern rainforests. The tropics produce plants with large, thick leaves, from the wide, fluffy leaves of teak trees to long and sleek coconut leaves, and smooth and waxy banana leaves. They lend themselves to wrapping and covering things. For example, the thatch on the roof of Thai farmers' huts is typically made of overlapping strips of *nipa* palm leaves, while an overlay of dried teak leaves, looking like big brown tobacco leaves, covers windows and gates.

Thailand benefited from the virtuosic qualities of banana leaves: water-resistant and foldable like paper, they can be cut into strips or folded into patterns like origami. These leaves, which are fairly waterproof, and therefore can be used as wrappings to keep the contents dry, came to feature in food as well.

Making a *baisri* flower offering: (*left*) fold pieces of banana leaf into triangles; (*centre*) combine the folded leaves into 'wings'; (*right*) a spire capped by a hard-boiled egg forms a completed *baisri*.

Here, Thai flowers diverge from the flowers of North Asia, which have a lot to do with vases they're put in. In Japan, when you study *ikebana*, a great deal of the focus is on baskets of bamboo, or pots of ceramic, lacquer or bronze. Flowers are just a part of what's going on: the container is half of the effect.

With *krathong*, there's no bamboo, ceramic or bronze – there's just flowers and leaves. You start on a flat plate or a bowl (or a slab of sliced banana tree trunk) and you build

Grand *baisri*: created for 2002 ceremony at the City Pillar.

upwards. It's incremental, put together leaf by leaf, folded edge by folded edge, like the bricks forming the indented pedestal of a Khmer temple.

In the flower class of the Bangkok arts programme, we learned that the temple tower being created, whether large or small, is always the same: a re-creation of sacred Mount Meru. In *baisri*, rising cones and extensions of folded bamboo leaves create the details of Mount Meru and its surroundings. One finishes it off with flowers, garlands and symbolic foods such as cucumbers and eggs.

This is the layout of Angkor Wat and also the layout of Wat Arun in Bangkok. In fact, Wat Arun, with its flowery surface of crockery and folded indentations, actually looks like a giant *baisri*. Even the simplest little *baisri* is still a Mount Meru, and as such a shadow of Indra hovers over it. Every time someone creates a *baisri* offering, they're building the mountain at the centre of the world.

Baisri and their related art, flower garlands, grow from the repetition of details – a typically Thai approach to art. You can see the same approach in *benjarong* ceramics, where an artisan covers the surface in ring after ring of small flower-like patterns combined to make one large geometry.

The same thing happens with *baisri*: leaf folded on leaf, interspersed with bits of red, white, purple and yellow from flower petals or tiny buds. Eventually the ensemble grows into an organic form. The Thais stitch leaves and petals together to form huge imaginary flowers. Unreal flowers, such as never were seen on land or sea.

The aim is to produce an object that's way beyond

Folded lotus buds: (*left*) lotus bud with outer petals folded under;
(*right*) folded lotuses float in a basin of water.

nature. Flowers from an alternative universe. The Thais apply their taste for turning nature into fantasy even with a single flower, when they take a lotus bud, and fold back the petals, one after another, until the luscious interior of the flower is revealed – surrounded by a collar of folded petals. No lotus ever naturally grew this way.

People vie in national competitions for the most elaborate *baisri*, and at certain Bangkok temples you can see magnificent ones that must have taken dozens of people many hours to create. Within the Grand Palace, a group of ladies labour daily on producing hundreds of floral objects consumed by Bangkok's many royal establishments.

On the street, garland sellers feed a voracious public appetite for offerings for homes, temples and Brahma shrines, as well as tuktuks and taxis, where you will often see a garland dangling over the dashboard. Flowers feature in dance, where Khon (classical theatre) performers suspend garlands from their crowns; and explosively, once a year, on the autumn festival of Loy Krathong, when millions of people float *krathong* (many made at home) in rivers, canals and lakes.

On Loy Krathong night, as you wander the streets, you come across a bewildering variety of *krathong*, each more colourful than the next, with central spires flanked by spiky and feathery additions. The only other Asian nation with a similar love of flowers is Bali, yet compared to Bangkok's finesse of detail, and its wild flourish of originality, Bali finishes only second.

Bangkok could never be called a 'garden city'. That name belongs deservedly to Singapore, which plants trees along roadways and then tends them with loving care, unlike in Bangkok, which has spent the last few decades cutting down trees and lopping off branches. In the place of greenery, Bangkok is busily erecting concrete structures that quickly blacken with mould in the damp

Loy Krathong night: *krathong* floating on the Chao Phraya River.

tropical climate. Even the sleekly designed sky train is looking slightly worn as it enters its third decade. Nevertheless, sprinkled over the grimy clutter of the city is a fairy dust of *baisri*, *krathong*, garlands and carved fruit.

Contemporary Flowers

As we can see from the word *baisri*, which is originally Khmer, Thai flowers originated outside Thailand. The concept goes back thousands of years to India (via Java and Angkor). Yet while the origins are ancient, Thai flowers have been the most successfully modernized of all the arts. This is because of the structural, geometrical side of Thai flowers.

Out of Bangkok comes one of the world's leading flower artists, Sakul Intakul. Sakul trained as an engineer, and he uses this as the basis for his approach. He takes materials such as banana leaves and orchids and builds them into 'structures' that can fit in with either a minimalist apartment or a banquet table for state guests. At the Sukhothai Hotel, you can see his framework of open bronze rectangles, inspired by pagodas, inset with changing arrangements of lotuses and rushes.

Flowers tell us where we are in the world. Hawaiian plumaria, Scottish thistles, Japanese cherry blossoms thrive in certain temperature, seasonal and rainfall patterns, which, in the case of Bangkok, are tropical. This brings us to a definitive aspect of Bangkok life, so obvious

Contemporary *baisri* by Sakul Intakul.

that writers and guidebooks mention it only in passing: it's hot.

Singapore manages an average temperature lower than Bangkok, even though it's several hundred kilometres further south and sits right on the equator. Bangkok's high thermometer readings arise from the swampy delta in which the city sits, not quite close enough to the sea to be cooled by ocean breezes; plus a 'heat island' effect caused by the cutting of trees in the city centre and replacing them with reflective glass and concrete.

One of the first things that every tourist does in Bangkok is visit the Grand Palace. At the Temple of the

Emerald Buddha, one learns of the three sets of golden raiment with which the King adorns the Emerald Buddha: one for each of the three seasons: hot, rainy and cool. Having just three seasons is alien to Westerners and verges on shocking to Japanese, for whom the concept of four seasons has almost religious value.

The three seasons are an artificial distinction in Bangkok because there's really just one never-ending season (warm), with varying degrees of heat and damp. In November and December, the temperature dips now and then a few degrees, and on those days the locals gambol in long-sleeved shirts, jackets and scarves. It's the only time they can show off their winter fashion. My friends all come down with terrible fevers and colds.

When rain comes it's never the slow drizzle that hangs darkly over Tokyo or London. Suddenly the heavens open, and giant droplets of rain fall so fiercely that you can hardly see more than a few feet ahead. Within minutes the streets are flooded (although Bangkok seems to be draining better these days). While the rain is pouring down, you have no choice but to sit it out. An hour or two later the storm winds down, then all of a sudden the rain lifts, and the city goes back to normal.

The heat means that Bangkok is not much of a walking city, despite the delights promised by many a Bangkok guidebook. There's not enough shade, and a few hours under the blazing sun is enough to leave you exhausted and wilted. Thais seem to have adapted to it. I'm always amazed at how crisp and fresh my Thai friends look after they've been out on a hot day; five minutes outdoors, and the sweat is running down my face, and my clothes are hopelessly wrinkled.

The legendary bad traffic is in fact not much worse than Tokyo, but sitting in that traffic for hours in the glaring sun makes it seem much worse. On the other hand, apartment buildings with rooftop pools, open-air restaurants at the top of skyscrapers, the marketplace of Chatuchak with thousands of open-air shops – it's only possible because of the heat. Add an extra wintry season, and it would kill the *sanuk*.

It's no accident that much of the fun and celebration in Bangkok takes place in the cool of the night,

Phuangmalai garlands.

whether it's the fireworks of New Year's Eve or the twinkling lights of the floating *krathong* on Loy Krathong.

One of the hallmarks of Bangkok is good building illumination. Restaurants and hotels light up pathways and windows with a gusto you would find in few cities of the world. People take pains to create a special effect, from candle-lit niches at restaurants to the avenue of trees draped in fairy lights leading from Sathorn to the Sukhothai Hotel. It works because Bangkok as a whole is a rather dark city, so good lighting stands out. The drab concrete-and-wire conglomeration that makes up most of the city disappears into the shadows.

Recent governments have been cracking down on Bangkok's late-night ways, on the grounds that going to sleep early is a hallowed Thai tradition. Actually, it's a Chinese businessman's tradition. Bangkok, and royal capitals before it, always functioned most effectively at night.

My favourite market in Bangkok trades mainly at night. It's the flower market at Pak Khlong Talad. Plants do not well survive the heat of the day, so flower vendors do most of their business after the sun sets. Pak Khlong Talad runs for several city blocks, surely the largest daily flower market in the world. This is where you will see piled up on the kerbside the flowers that reappear across the city the next morning as *baisri* in temples and floral arrangements in hotels, shops and homes.

A Night in Himmaphan

When I give a party at my apartment at Soi 16, we go out the night before to Pak Khlong Talad to buy flowers. Vendors start opening their stalls in the afternoon, but the market really comes alive after nightfall and is at its best around midnight. Heaped high are bundles of lotuses wrapped in wide lotus leaves, piles of orchids in every colour, plastic bags of jasmine kept cool with crushed ice, clusters of leaves (banana, *bai toey*, staghorn fern), chrysanthemums and ginger stalks two metres high with pink and orange spiky flowers dangling down on droopy tendrils.

Amidst this 'urban jungle', ladies set up stands where they weave flower petals into garlands simple and complex. You can buy slabs of chopped-up banana trunk (the traditional base of a *krathong*), decorative fruits such as dragon-fruit and squashes, and all manner of forest produce such as *kra-jiap* ('rosella'), a purple flower that looks like it came out of *The Little Shop of Horrors*.

We bundle all this into one (or two) taxis, bring it home, and then we spend the rest of the night arranging it – which in Thailand means cutting, folding, bending or floating in water basins. One of my Thai staff, a young man named Soe, has become our resident Thai flower designer.

Soe fills a wide flat bowl full of water to the brim and

Imaginary Himmaphan flowers – floating arrangements by Soe:
folded lotuses at centre, surrounded by rose petals, orchids,
symbidium, tiny *dok phut* buds and pandanus leaves.

in the centre sets a white lotus with folded-back petals. He surrounds that with a floating layer of orchids, rose petals and four slim pandanus leaves, like setting a jewel in a ring. Each arrangement is a new turn of a kaleidoscope, with petals and leaves shifting to reveal new patterns, each one a weird new flower in its own right.

Soe's sunflowers hail from the mythical Himmaphan forest, full of hodge-podge flora and fauna. Sometimes I reflect on why it is that the Thais chose Himmaphan as the ideal locus for their art. Himmaphan exists as a concept in India and China, but nobody paid much attention to it. Yet in Thailand, out of all the many realms of heaven, earth and hell described in the Traiphum cosmology, artists chose Himmaphan as their favourite place to sculpt and paint.

The exotica of Himmaphan surround us wherever you see traditional decor: elephants with wings, deer with demon masks, hallucinatory flowers. The mythical forest suited the Thai temperament.

The next night, when guests arrive, the house has taken on the 'Thai look'. It also takes on the sweet smell of *jampi* and *jampa*, large and small varieties of fragrant flowers originally from India.

Over by the windows stand the tall ginger stalks with drooping blossoms; garlands dangle in front of things with spirits in them such as dance masks and Buddhist paintings; Soe's colourful creations bloom on stands and tables. During the evening some of the guests might reveal themselves as composites of graceful animals and naughty angels. For one night, with a little extra help from music and wine, we can believe that we're dwelling in Himmaphan.

Not that we ever really left it.

Dance
ระบำรำฟ้อน

12

เขตพัฒน์พงศ์

Whenever I see any sort of dance, I feel I've had a wasted life. Dance – watching it, because I could never perform it – has been a lifelong passion.

In Japan, this led me into the Kabuki world, and I spent years lurking around the backstage, soaking up everything I could about dance, costume and the actors themselves. In Bangkok, I discovered dance rather late.

Like many tourists, my first memory of seeing Thai dance is of the girls who perform at the Erawan Shrine to Brahma. Some time later, a friend took me to see the dinner show at the Oriental Hotel restaurant across the Chao Phraya River, and this is when I first heard the word 'Khon', Thailand's masked drama, centred on the Ramakien epic. The shimmering costumes and head-dresses lent these dances a glamorous air, but I couldn't shake the feeling that I was somehow missing the point.

I went to see Khon at universities and shows at Sala Chalermkrung Royal Theatre, complete with laser beams and dancers flying through the air. Feeling guilty as my eyelids began to droop, I looked around and noticed plenty of other people nodding off to sleep too.

The epiphany about Khon came in 1998, when I rented Khun Santi's complex of wooden Thai pavilions at Ladphrao. One evening a friend brought over a troupe of dancers and puppeteers to perform on the wooden plat-form at the Ladphrao house. With them were the dance master Khru Kai and costume designer Peeramon Chom-dhavat, and this time, Khon worked its magic.

Arising inside the palace, Khon was performed in confined spaces before a small audience so close that they could almost touch the artists. As a result, the eye is drawn to tiny detail, whether it's threads of embroi-dery on the costume, or the fine turn of a wrist. That night, seeing Khon in the intimate setting of a small wooden pavilion, I finally could understand why the kings and princes of old took such a passionate interest in their dance troupes.

I set out to learn more. It wasn't easy. In Japan, at Kabukiza Theatre in Tokyo, they sell programmes with an outline of the story and lease 'earphone guides' that explain, in Japanese and in English, the fine points of costume and gesture, as well as the background of the actors.

In Thailand, by contrast, one sets out into unknown territory without a map. English-language explanations rarely get beyond basics, such as 'The one wearing a white mask is the monkey Hanuman.' Mostly, there is no explanation in any language, even Thai.

Nor is Khon easy to see. The schedule of the National Theatre is a closely guarded secret. The old Sala Chalermkrung Royal Theatre near Chinatown stages Khon shows for tourists – sometimes. The National Culture Centre occasionally puts on a lavish production. But, as of 2021, there is still no regular venue where one can reliably go and see Khon, so finding it is a matter of hit and miss.

Khloem

Khru Kai and Peeramon Chomdhavat became my guides. Their partnership dates back to the early 2000s, when Peeramon set out to revive old costume. Peeramon's background lay in Western ballet, not Khon. However, he had loved Thai dance since childhood, and it disturbed him when he saw the stiff and tinsely-looking costumes of present-day Khon. He knew it must once have been better.

Khru Kai (Surat Jongda) hails from Khonkaen province in the Northeast (*Kai,* meaning chicken, is a typical

Thai nickname; the word *khru*, derived from the Sanskrit *guru*, meaning 'teacher', is an honorific for artists or professors). He started dancing at fourteen, came to Bangkok at the age of nineteen and rose to become a teacher at the national specialty college for dance and music.

Peeramon and Khru Kai researched old photographs and pored over jewellery and brocades in private collections. Peeramon began embroidering, using gold and silver instead of aluminium, and insetting into the patterns iridescent blue beetle's wings, instead of plastic rhinestones. With Khru Kai's dancers he began to turn Khon on to a new path. It was those beautiful costumes that I saw that first night at Ladphrao.

Under Peeramon and Kai's tutelage I went to see quite a lot of Khon, and I learned that the stage is a numinous place belonging to the gods, not to people. The purpose of Khon is to lead the viewer into a mythical realm. Dancing for centuries by flares and moonlight in the royal courts, Khon dancers evolved a turn of the neck, a twist of the wrist, elegant forms that belong to angels and devas, not human beings. Repetition of these forms in subtly varying tempos can lead the viewer to an almost hypnotic trance. Sometimes you hear this described as *khloem*, a day-dreaming state not quite in this world.

Khon as we see it now differs widely from Khon of a hundred years ago, and we can only guess what form it took before the fall of Ayutthaya. Peeramon and Khru Kai struggled to explain the niceties to me. Khon went through phases: at the beginning it was performed only by men. Later, there were all-female troupes performing inside the palace, and all-male troupes performing outside the palace. By the mid-twentieth century, these had merged, producing what most people call Khon today. The details of who wore a mask and in what era, or which genres men or women performed, are all quite technical. What did come across is that the art form has been in constant flux, with major changes taking place quite recently.

Over time, I began to see Khon's typical forms and costumes in almost every situation that's officially 'Thai', beginning with *The Churning of the Sea of Milk* installation at Bangkok International Airport. It's difficult to get through a day in Bangkok without running across an advertisement with a model wearing a golden Khon-style crown, or a poster of dancers posed in front of ancient ruins.

Khon, of course, accounts for only a tiny fraction of Thai dance. A huge range of folk forms exist, from the *fon phii* (shaman dances) of the North to *ramwong* ('circle dancing'), which you find across the country. In *ramwong*, performed at festivals and parties, people dance in a circle, waving their hands while making the two basic gestures of Thai dance: *wong* (thumb bent inwards over the palm, four fingers curving outwards) and *jiib* (thumb and index fingers touching, three fingers curving outwards).

University students dance for the annual *wai khru* (homage to teachers) ceremonies at the beginning of the school year. At shrines such as the Erawan Brahma and the City Pillar, supplicants whose wishes have come true engage a troupe of dancers to perform in gratitude.

Mekhala and Ramasuun: classical Thai dance in which the demon Ramasuun tries to steal a magic gem from the angel Mekhala.

And occasionally, dancers perform for me. I used to love to invite dancers to the old Thai house complex at Ladphrao, where they danced against the background of pointed roofs and a giant fan palm. As you watched, lulled by the rhythms of a *piphaat* orchestra, you fell into a state of meditative *khloem*. You really did feel that you were in the presence of angels.

Nowadays, the dancers perform at my apartment. It doesn't have quite the mystique of the Ladphrao house, but the dancers still work their magic. One of my favourite pieces is *Mekhala and Ramasuun*. Mekhala, a heavenly goddess, is playing with her magic gem, which flashes as she twirls it. Ramasuun, a demon, tries to steal it from her and, at the climactic moment, he hurls his jewelled axe, which crashes onto the floor. The crash of the axe and the sparkle of the gem are thunder and lightning. That's the folk tale. At the higher level, the gem's sparkle is a glimpse of the divine.

Dance as Painting

When Indian dance moved across Southeast Asia, it ended up focusing on the Ramayana epic, which was important in India, but never to the degree that it became in Southeast Asia. Especially in Thailand, where the kings named themselves after the hero Rama, the Ramayana's tale of the war between good and evil became the saga of the nation.

One curious change from India was the role of puppets. To a surprising degree, in Southeast Asia, puppets came first, and only later were their movements copied by human beings. That's where we get elbows and fingers that curve backwards, necks that swivel in impossible angles, and stop-motion poses at the height of the drama.

Since dancers expressed the glamour of the royal court, they came to be draped in gold brocades and spangled with bejewelled rings and bracelets. Curving fingers, puppet-like gestures, masks and crowns, glittering costumes – all these combined to to make dance exquisite, gem-like, unearthly.

Dance in Thailand was a vision of heaven. Actually dance was a *painting* of heaven. The first thing that visitors see when visiting Bangkok is the Ramayana murals at the gallery of the Temple of the Emerald Buddha inside the Grand Palace. Angels, demons and monkeys wear not human faces, but theatrical masks; they're posed as if they were actors on the stage: fingers twisted backwards, warriors with legs raised high in the heroic postures of Khon, courtiers prostrated on the ground with legs folded under, like dancers paying respect to the King.

The embroidery on dance costumes, the curving flanges of the crowns – these are *Lai Thai* designs as you see in murals. In the bigger theatres, Khon performances reach their climax in tableaux of golden chariots with dozens of actors posed in arrested motion, just like the Ramayana paintings at the palace.

You can see links to architecture too, or rather, architecture as it appears in paintings. On their heads, Khon dancers wear *chadaa* crowns, which are the spires above a painted palace or a pagoda, while from their shoulders rise epaulets evoking rising temples eaves. The dancer is a pavilion in motion, a moving Mount Meru.

I came to realize that when you watch Khon dancers, you have entered into a painting, and this explains the sense of stillness that comes across in Khon. Each gesture is a perfect pose that you could frame as a single scene. Often, to bring home the beauty of the pose, the dancers

Chadaa crown: a miniature palace spire rises
from the crown of a Khon dancer.

will actually freeze motion, flattened for an instant back
into the painting that they're a part of. Time literally
stops. At those moments you can feel that sense of *khloem*
that princes of old sought in their royal troupes.

Hands and Fingers

Thailand belongs to 'Indianized Southeast Asia', in contrast to Vietnam, Japan and Korea, where China dominated.
For dance this makes a huge difference because India,
unlike China, loved the human body.

In India, naked male and female dancers cavort in

temple friezes; Lord Shiva, also naked, whirls ecstatically with one leg raised as Lord of the Dance. Dance and the body are divine.

This was definitely not the case in China or Japan, where the human body disappears within layers of robes and kimono. In the old days the Chinese and Japanese authorities viewed dance performances as vulgar. They ranked Peking Opera and Kabuki actors as lower than beggars, and there are numerous recorded cases of dancers being banished or even executed for stepping out of line.

In India, dancers were divinities, and when this idea travelled to ancient Java and Cambodia, dancers came to be revered as gods and goddesses protecting the royal court. Heavenly dancers feature in the carvings at Borobudur, and hundreds of glorious *apsara* pose elegantly on the bas-reliefs of Angkor Wat.

Along the way, possibly beginning in Java, something new happened: the fingers bent backwards. Thailand later carried this to the ultimate extreme, with the fingernail extensions that typify Thai dance in the eyes of the world. The curved fingers tell us that the dancer is not human; he or she is an angel.

Emphasis on hands and fingers is perhaps the single biggest difference between dance in the West and in the East. In India, each finger gesture, or *mudra*, expressed the power of a god. These *mudras* speak to us like codewords in a language. As Indian dance moved east and north, and the fingers bent backwards, most of the meanings of the *mudra* disappeared.

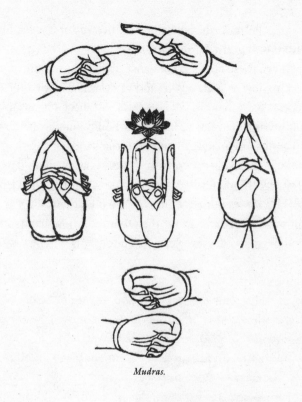

Mudras.

The two basic hand gestures of Thai dance: (*right*) *wong* – wrist and fingers bent back, thumb turned inwards; (*left*) *jiib* – thumb and index finger touching, three fingers splayed outwards.

221

In Thailand, what remained of the *mudra* was the two basic hand gestures, *jiib* and *wong*.

From these forms, Thai dance acquired its infinite variety. As in *Lai Thai* design and in flowers, the two forms repeat, merge and mingle, and as the dancer's hands turn and twist from high to low, in and out, complex patterns emerge – attenuated and elegant, the hands of angels.

The emphasis on curving fingers is what gives dance from Japan down to Java its distinctive lilt. It's not a trivial lilt. It's essential. I think it's truly addictive. There must be something about the waving of those hands and fingers that releases pleasure endorphins in the brain.

Contemporary Thai dance with fingernail extensions by Ronnarong Khampha.

Once you've discovered it, you simply cannot live without it. The artist Symon of Bali used to say, 'Life stops being wonderful – unless there are dancers.'

Eros

Khon has a masculine and feminine side. The feminine appears in the delicately turned head and curved fingers of the gentle hero and heroine; the masculine can be seen in the virile outstretched legs and muscular hand gestures of the demon or the acrobatics of the Monkey. These come from the martial arts practices of the palace guard, who were the first, according to tradition, to perform Khon. As a result, Khon's poses have much to do with swordsmanship and even *muay thai* kickboxing.

It's no accident that the masculine and feminine come together in dance, because dance and music are so closely linked to sex, as the ancient Indians well understood. That's why the elite of China and Japan disapproved of actors in the old days – they saw acting as one step away from selling one's body. In fact, in pre-modern times, Kabuki dancers and Chinese opera singers did sleep with patrons.

In Thailand, by contrast, dancers in the palace had a high status, sometimes being royal consorts, or even princes. But by the simple fact of being the human body in motion, dance everywhere in the world carries erotic overtones.

223

The expression of Eros in dance, across East Asia, differs from the West in that it tends to be androgynous. Men playing female roles are core to Kabuki with its *onnagata* and Peking Opera with its *dan*. Burma has its transvestite actors and shamans.

Khon had been all-male at its origin, with men playing women. Later, when women did palace dance, they performed male roles. With all this blending going on, lines between yin and yang blurred, with male roles taking on feminine delicacy.

The lower garment of male roles, the *jongkrabane*, filled out until it became a wide, stiff 'bustle', exaggerating the hips and making the men appear slightly more

Phra Ram, the hero of the Ramakien epic, in classical Khon dance pose.

female. Make-up in Khon was once more abstract and mask-like, but in recent times it has become feminized, with lots of eye-shadow and red lipstick. A 'beauty queen' principle seems to have taken over. When I first saw a male heroic role performed as a solo dance, I thought this lovely creature with glistening red lips and flowers in her hair, must be the heroine!

In classical Khon, the Demon, wearing a fearsome mask, stamps and postures with masculine vigour. Nothing androgynous in that role. The hero, Phra Ram, however, waves his hands as softly as a delicate maiden. In fact, the actor who plays Phra Ram might be a delicate maiden, or a lady of mature years, since women sometimes perform the role. Likewise, either a man or a woman might play the heroine.

One is tempted to think beyond Khon, to the androgynous nature of Thai society in general, another similarity shared with Japan. The best-known Bangkok symbol of that are the *katoey* (male-to-female transsexuals). If you live in Bangkok, *katoey* make a visible mark on society. Many work as sales staff in hotels and restaurants. Large theatres such as Tiffany in Pattaya and Mambo in Bangkok feature all-*katoey* cabaret revues, much frequented by Chinese and Korean tourists. *Katoey* star in their own beauty contests, judged by society figures. Surely no country in the world gives such an honoured role to its 'lady-boys' (as they are called in Thailand).

If you walk along Sukhumvit Road late at night you'll sometimes catch sight of a foreign man walking hand in hand with a *katoey*, and on occasion you wonder if he's fully aware that his partner is not – originally – a woman. The *katoey* are a favourite subject for Western novelists writing about Bangkok, and many a mystery plot turns on a twist of gender identity.

Actually, 'cross-dressing' did not come naturally to Thailand. How can you dress like the opposite sex if both sexes dress the same? In the nineteenth century, foreign visitors noted that both men and women wore their hair short, a sarong for the lower body, and often the upper body unclothed. When the upper body was clothed, similarities became all the closer. Diplomats complained that at official dinners they couldn't tell the men apart from the women.

Perhaps because of the loose boundaries between genders, not only *katoey*, but also gay life seems more prominent in Bangkok than elsewhere, adding to the city's dubious reputation abroad. Lesbians (often called 'toms' and 'dees') also make a strong presence in Bangkok, as you can see if you spend an afternoon at the youth area of Siam Square.

Magical Trees
Maybe it's part of being in the Himmaphan forest. One of the popular trees of Himmaphan is the Makaripon tree, from which hangs fruits that grow into beautiful ladies. If trees in Himmaphan sprout ladies, and angels spring out of vines, why shouldn't men become women

and vice-versa? Or it could be due to the Thai sense of the cycle of rebirth and inevitable karma. You were born to be what you are, so you might as well enjoy it.

While recently Taiwan has started to catch up, Bangkok has had for decades the most extensive gay scene in all of Asia. Discos accommodating hundreds of people pulse until late in the night. Cameron McMillan, my young Kiwi friend, on his first visit to a gay disco in Silom Soi 2, took one look at the crowds of men and could barely contain himself. 'When I die, I want to come here!' he said.

Another of the legends associated with Himmaphan has it that inside the forest there is a magical Chommanat

Makaripon tree with hanging lady fruit.

tree, whose blossoms are so intoxicating that all who inhale them must immediately go off and have sex with whatever is closest at hand. That's what gave birth to the cross-beings found in Himmaphan: bird-monkeys, lion-snakes, angel-fish and so forth.

Sometimes I feel that there's a great Chommanat tree looming over Bangkok. As to why it flourishes here more than elsewhere, there's the lack of a Judaeo-Christian-Islamic tradition of moral disapproval. Also, a weaker impact from Chinese paternalism and the Confucian work ethic. The lack of clear lines between genders. And finally, Bangkok's place as a crossroads with a broad mix of races and ethnicities.

The list of ingredients goes on: Bangkok is a holiday destination filled with lusty visitors from all over the world. The 'culture of negotiation', which tends not to stick to the letter of the law, allows all sorts of venues to exist that might have a harder time in a stricter society. Top these off with the Thai smile and warm weather, and the combination makes Bangkok – for men, women and everything in between – the sexiest place on earth.

This is not news. You can hardly pick up a book about Bangkok by a foreign author, Westerner or Japanese, that is not strongly coloured, if not obsessed, by this aspect of the city. For many Westerners, especially women, the ready availability of commercial sex makes Thailand seem anything but 'sexy', even for some, abhorrent.

Yet despite the festival atmosphere at Silom, Thai society is hardly the open sexual paradise that many foreigners imagine. This is another of those illusions propagated by the surface gloss of *sanuk*. Young ladies of good families are educated to be sexually quite conservative. Gays often do not come out to their parents, and many stay permanently in the closet for fear of being discriminated against at work.

In fact, there's a strong streak of puritanism running through Thai society. Reinforced by the rituals of *marayaat* etiquette, a love of *riaproy* – doing things properly – runs deep in society. Austere Chinese morality, which frowns on sensual indulgence, plays a role, and you can also see vestiges of colonial Western values from the nineteenth century.

The biggest influence of all is the long decades of military rule, when rulers insisted that people conform to officially mandated standards, like wearing a hat to work. You won't find in Bangkok the open flaunting of sex that you find in Japan, such as newspapers sporting photos of naked-breasted adult video stars, which salarymen peruse in the train on their way home from work.

Periodically, the Thai ministries of education or culture, or one of the other boards in charge of mandating 'Thai identity', starts up an anti-sexuality campaign, which could take the form of a crackdown on 'immodest behaviour', which has been interpreted to mean strapless dresses.

Underlying this is a sense of revulsion that society feels against the more obvious signs of Bangkok's booming sex business. It gives the city an unsavoury air and is a source of embarrassment internationally. Prostitution continues to thrive anyway, partly due to poverty, of course, and partly due to the fact that the Thais don't take it as seriously as Westerners do. They see it (as do the Japanese) as a biological urge and they don't much concern themselves about it, so long as it keeps a low profile.

The Weimar Republic Theory of Bangkok

Part of what excited Cameron so much at the disco was the smiles all around. He had the feeling that he was welcome, a feeling he hadn't so much had when he lived in Tokyo. In another part of town, fat old Westerners with slender young bar girls on their laps were getting the same feeling. The big welcome makes Bangkok a lodestone for males (not only ageing, but young as well; not only white, but Japanese, Chinese, Nigerians, Arabs). When they die, this is where they all want to go.

Ironically, openness to foreigners works against Bangkok in the eyes of the world. Prostitution is a far larger business in Japan than it is in Thailand, but it bothers foreign visitors and journalists much less, if at all. One doesn't often see an outraged article about the scandalous sexuality of modern Tokyo. This is because most of the sex is not accessible to foreigners; they just don't see it. In fact, much of Thai prostitution is also hidden. Far more goes on in massage parlours and hairdressers than meets the eye in the go-go bars of Patpong – and the customers are in the majority Thai, not foreign.

I have what I call 'the Weimar Republic theory' of

Bangkok. As dramatized in the movie *Cabaret*, there was a moment of sinful freedom in Berlin during the Weimar Republic (1919–33). It was the era of Kurt Weill's bittersweet music and Christopher Isherwood's novels and stories. By the mid-1930s, the Nazis had stamped it out, and eventually all that remained was a legend of 'Berlin in the 1920s'. Those who experienced it spent the rest of their lives telling others of the wild days that were now gone for ever.

The outrageous forms that prostitution has taken in Bangkok (sex shows, go-go bars with half-naked boys or girls gyrating on tables) are quietly slipping away from view. Slowly but surely the high waters of the sinful Bangkok of yesteryear are receding, and those days will fade into legend, just as 1920s Berlin did. One day we'll tell our children or grandchildren, 'This is what you used to be able to see in Bangkok . . .'

Patpong is no longer where the action is. The tourists who throng Patpong are there mostly to buy souvenir trinkets; few venture into the sex establishments. It will not be long before Patpong is lined more with coffee shops and galleries than with go-go bars. Given rising real estate values, the Patpongpanit family (who own the whole block) might simply sell it all off to be redeveloped as a mall.

Meanwhile, there's a new open sexuality among the youth, which alarms conservative elements in society. Back in the 1980s and early 1990s, Rome Club on Silom Soi 4 was one of the few places where young urban professionals hung out. Since then, nightlife has exploded into a wide range of venues all across town.

Youngsters dance the night away at the huge discos at RCA (Royal City Avenue); gays go to Silom Soi 2; and a mixed crowd fills the pubs on Silom Soi 4. Fancy nightclubs on Soi Thonglor attract a well-heeled clientele. Thaniya Road appeals to the Japanese, but also features British pubs. Meanwhile, young Thais and foreigners mingle in the nightspots of Banglampoo, the backpacker district.

As late as the mid-1990s, boys and girls rarely held hands in public. Handholding was mostly a boy-boy or girl-girl thing. Outside their homes, people shunned physical contact. Now this is all changing, and dance in the discos has a lot to do with it.

Resisting all this fun and freedom are the forces of *riaproy*, propriety. The authorities see dance as dangerous and have done their best to restrict it, by tightening the zoning for entertainment districts, and requiring clubs to close earlier and earlier. Bangkok is already more restrictive than Singapore or Tokyo when it comes to mandated closing times.

In Bangkok, whenever you find *sanuk*, *riaproy* is not far behind. These two are the never-separated dancers of Bangkok life.

An Australian woman friend of mine complained, 'Bangkok is Boy's Town.' This was true, because women had little choice. Thai men were free to have a wandering eye; women were not. The laws changed to favour monogamy, but the culture lagged.

In the process, to redress polygamy, Thai laws became increasingly feminist. The drift has been to treat women better. Over time this has had an effect, and today Thai women play a stronger role in the society than their counterparts in Japan. They are going to universities and running companies. Women are working away from home, and millions have migrated from villages into the city, where they escape prying eyes of neighbours and family. Impacted by Western ideas of the equality of the sexes, women are taking their lives into their own hands.

My guess at what is going on is that we see in Bangkok a remnant of the matriarchal society that the Thais brought down with them through the valleys of the Mekong. The female principle ruled, and in some way continues to do so. Previously, the female principle ran the household, and the male principle controlled society. Nowadays, however, the power of women extends increasingly into the public realm.

The growing freedom of women in Thailand, combined with androgyny and *sanuk*, would seem to be a formula for 'anything goes'. However, that very freedom of women acts as a brake on the free-wheeling male promiscuity of the past. Balanced against *sanuk* is the impetus towards *riaproy* as society grows more middle-class and internationalized.

Sanuk is to be found laughing, drinking and dancing at every party. But along with him, he's brought his elegantly dressed companion, *riaproy*. She sits coolly in the corner, keeping a sharp eye on what goes on, making sure that nothing gets too far out of hand.

Neo-Bangkok
นวมหานคร

13

เขตบางกอกใหม่

T he historian Kenneth Clark proclaimed, 'Poverty is the patron goddess of beauty.' He was referring to Venice, which lost all its money in the nineteenth century and therefore didn't have the resources to tear down the old town and build a modern city, as Paris and London did; as a result, the wonder that is Venice survived.

In Asia, money has played a dual role. As nations rush to modernize, money at first destroys and ravages old cities and nature. People confuse 'westernization' with 'modernization', and so they see their own tradition as backward, something to be ashamed of.

Later, a turning point arrives. Once people have reached a comfortable standard of living, they start to revalue their native culture, and money then enables a cultural rebirth. This is what happened in Japan after the 1970s, with the revival of Kabuki and rise of designers such as Issey Miyake.

Thailand, when I started visiting back in the 1970s, was still in the traditional phase, despite the fact that Bangkok was already a busy commercial city, and the kings of Thailand had been westernizing the country for a century. The Goddess of Poverty still ruled and held her protecting hand over wooden towns and pristine rice paddies. I remember going to the floating market in 1973 and being so overwhelmed by the placid beauty of the scene that I wept. Now, of course, one could only weep at the tourist frenzy that it has become.

On the train from Bangkok to Chiang Mai, just outside of town, rice paddies came into view, and from there you saw an uninterrupted landscape of green fields, interspersed with villages and temples, all the way up to the north. The *sois* off Bangkok's main roads had a leafy, even rural, feel to them.

Then, like Japan, it began to change. In Thailand, the big economic growth started two decades later than Japan, picking up steam in the 1990s. Overnight, the city went from verdant *sois* and quaint shophouses to a conglomeration of highways, high-rise condos and malls.

The Revival of Khon and Puppets

By the late 1990s, traditional arts were reaching their nadir, and classical masked dance in particular, was hard hit. Khon relied on a dwindling coterie of grey-haired matrons, and in the process Khon froze. 'Freezing' is a common syndrome that happens when a traditional art survives only as a form, and people start to forget about its original purpose.

Once upon a time, kings and princes draped their dancers in brocades woven from the finest gold threads. They commissioned masks from masters who would meditate at each step of the creation, and they adorned the performers with jewelled diadems that were marvels of the goldsmith's art. In the postwar years, embroidery degraded in quality, and the costumes took on the tinsely look that Khon usually has today. Mask-makers applied bright Western paints instead of old-style mineral pigments, so the masks too came to look more like cartoons than what they had once been: eerie avatars of the gods.

Meanwhile, the dance petrified. A few masters persevered in the palace and in the universities, but Khon in general fell into formula. Young Thais turned away,

Hun lakhorn lek puppets: three black-clad puppeteers manipulate the puppet while posing in step with the music.

being unable to find anything of value, and so Khon's audience shrank even further.

By the early 2000s, Thailand began to cross the line from being simply a poor Third World country to being a developed modern state. The transformation is, of course, far from complete. Millions still live in poverty, not only in the countryside but here in Bangkok. Nevertheless, many have now joined the middle class and, like the Japanese in the 1970s, they're ready to rediscover their own culture.

New times call for a rethink. Onisaburo, founder of

Oomoto, where we used to run the school of traditional arts, taught that the way forward was to go back. Not just back a little, but way, way, back. Onisaburo said: overleap recent eras, return to the arts to their ancient starting point. Brush away the 'dust' of recent years and go 'back to the origin' – and rebuild from there.

My guides to Khon, Peeramon and Khru Kai, in mining the past to create their new Khon costumes, have been doing just that. Their costumes, while based on old forms, transcend them, for they have the ability to choose the best from the world, and from within Thai history itself. They'll bring in a pattern they found in an old book, which hasn't been used in centuries – if it ever has been. Their costumes look old but are creatively new, quite likely more beautiful than anything seen in earlier times.

Thailand once had a number of puppet traditions, but by the mid-twentieth century, all of these were on the verge of extinction. In 1974, a puppeteer named Liew acquired one of the last surviving sets of *hun lakhon lek* (movable puppets). He came up with an approach inspired by Japanese Bunraku puppets, adapting his *hun lakhon lek* so as to be controlled by two or three black-clad puppeteers. In contrast to Bunraku, in which the puppeteers keep in the background, Liew made his puppeteers themselves a part of the dance, training them to step move with the elegant poses of Khon, so that puppeteer and puppet became one.

Today the troupe he founded performs nightly in downtown Bangkok, winning international prizes for its choreography and gaining fame as one of the cultural gems of Thailand.

Experimentation

Contemporary artists in Asia can go two routes: One is to pursue the conceptual art of New York and Beijing. Another is to take a unique quality from their own tradition and create something modern out of that.

My Malaysian friend Zul first opened my eyes to how it can be done. Zul trained in classical Malay dance, but he was at his best as an improvisational performer. I watched Zul climb and descend concrete staircases, balance on I-beams, wrap himself in plastic sheeting – all while twiddling his fingers like a Balinese dancer, or sliding his feet like a noble in an old Malay court. From Zul I saw how rich the resources of tradition could be for a modern Asian dancer.

From 1992 until it closed in 2014, the hot-spot for such experimentation in Bangkok was Patravadi Theatre, located across the river from the Grand Palace. Founded by actress Patravadi Mejudhon, the theatre sponsored a spectrum of Thai drama, from student shows to *Manohra* dancing from the South. Wealthy through her mother who ran the express boats on the Chao Phraya River, Patravadi subsidized the whole thing for years. She had no obligation to spend her fortune on the arts, and she's unusual in doing so; in fact, arts suffer badly in Bangkok for lack of patronage. While her theatre has closed, her disciples carry on as leaders in Thai performance art.

Amidst the experimentation at Patravadi and other venues, dancer Pichet Klunchun succeeded in making Khon truly contemporary. Pichet trained as a *yak* (demon) character in Khon, and he took the stamping and forceful arm gestures of the *yak* as his starting point. He bypassed the pretty feminine side of classical dance and went straight back to Khon's martial arts beginnings. With his athletically tempered body and stoic frame of mind, Pichet had the means to strip Khon down to its essence.

And that's what Pichet did. He stripped. Wearing only a sarong and an elephant mask, he painted his body white like a Butoh dancer, performing Khon in stark modern

Contemporary dance by Pichet Klunchun: wearing a sarong and an elephant mask, his body smeared with white powder, Pichet reinvents traditional dance in modern guise.

settings. You could see beyond the costume to the core physicality of the art. Which takes us all the way back to India's naked gods and goddesses where the whole thing began thousands of years ago. In focusing on Khon's martial arts aspect, Pichet found a way to make statements about Buddhist spirituality.

At other times, Pichet manages to insert a strong political message. Basing himself in tradition, but electrifyingly relevant to today's issues, Pichet has appeared at theatre festivals around the world, becoming one of Thailand's best-known performing artists.

The Thai renaissance, most of which bubbles up out of Bangkok, is not limited to performing arts. Sakul, the flower artist, has made an international reputation. Thai film has broken through with cinema directors such as award-winning Aphichatphong Wirasetthakun.

Unfortunately, Thailand suffers from censorship. The government meddles more and more, not only with political messages, but even with the look of the art itself.

Bureaucrats are imposing their idea of 'Thainess' on the nation, smoothing out regional styles in favour of official forms created in Bangkok. Where Thai arts once revelled in quirky variations, they're being 'cleaned up' and homogenized.

For the moment, censorship has had a sharpening effect, as artists find ways to evade or subtly ridicule officialdom. Repression keeps artists' eyes focused on social injustices that they might overlook in an easy-going bourgeois environment. Chinese film directors in the 1990s, ballet dancers from the Soviet Union – they all did their best work when struggling under an authoritarian regime. However, when the repressive powers of such a regime cross a certain line, as in China since the late 2010s, the artists, working within ever narrowing confines, start to lose their relevance. So far, this hasn't happened in Thailand, but it's a delicate balancing act.

In Bangkok, censorship standards are vague, leaving plenty of space to breathe, but at the same time lots of room for anyone to criticize the artist. As a journalist or artist, one must keep alert to the idea that people could take things the wrong way, especially with the growing emphasis on 'Thainess'. Self-censorship rules, and the trend is towards everyone becoming more careful, not less.

So far, modern design has fallen below the censorship radar, because designers have no interest in putting across a concept, political or not. Of all sectors, it's design that really thrives. Youth fashion at Siam Square can be fairly said to lead the Southeast Asian region. I have a friend in the fashion world from Jakarta who flies regularly to Bangkok to check out the latest in what Thai youth are wearing, which will later be repackaged back in Jakarta and Singapore.

Tourist Culture

At Chatuchak Market, or at upscale Gaysorn Plaza, you can see inventive Thai design in the making. Some designers take traditional craft (natural materials such as bamboo, lacquer or wickerwork) and reshape them in modern form. Others take the lines of *Lai Thai* patterns, and the vivid pinks and yellows that Thais so delight in, and transfer these to modern devices in plastic, aluminium or glass.

Bangkok offers a wider range of goods than in many other Asian places, because Thai designers can draw on a deep well of traditional themes, something they share with Japan. Japan and Thailand regularly come up with quirky new ideas you can't find in homogenized global culture. In this sense, Thailand is the Japan of Southeast Asia.

The reality is that much of the cultural revival is aimed at and supported by tourists, making the Thai renaissance as much about 'tourism' as it is about 'art'. This differs sharply with Japan, where tourism, until recently, was still a minor part of the economy. Japanese authorities believed that modern nations made things in factories, while poor countries relied on tourism. The opposite happened in Thailand, which is swamped all year round with tourists from every corner of the globe. Resorts and restaurants have found a voracious appetite for 'Thai-culture' events and amusements, and a thriving industry has grown up to feed that.

Thai culture has been chopped up and reassembled as 'show'. Bangkok hosts an endless parade of dance and culture spectacles, son et lumière, beauty pageants and historical musicals with casts of hundreds. It's where the real energies of the culture now flow, because this is where the budgets are. In the process, Thailand has become rather good at it.

Bangkok is the tourist city par excellence of East Asia, with the result that a lot of Bangkok culture is tourist culture. Tourists have created thriving enclaves in Patpong, Silom, the backpacker mecca of Khaosan Road in Banglampoo and Soi Thonglor, which is a twenty-four-hour foreigner promenade. It's because of the tourists that we have so many world-class restaurants and hotels to enjoy; not to mention the fun at Khaosan Road, and craft industries that would otherwise barely exist.

Until I began spending time regularly in Bangkok in the early 1990s, I had hardly ever given tourism a second thought. In Japan in those days it was largely irrelevant. However, tourism is now the biggest industry in the world, and its global impact is just beginning to be felt, with even Japan becoming dependent on tourism at the end of the 2010s. Bangkok lies on the front lines of the world tourist explosion; here you can observe the new global fusion taking place before your eyes.

Tourism is a double-edged sword. While it brings in income, it cheapens and degrades when the 'real thing' dies and tourist trinket-mongering takes its place – as in the floating market. The most extravagant shows can never take the place of the meditative beauty that was refined over centuries in Khon. That's why, in the end, it's important to preserve the real thing as the wellspring or 'origin' to which modern artists can always return for inspiration.

In China, relics of the past exist everywhere, refurbished and fitted out with museums and souvenir shops.

However, it's hard to find monuments that serve their original purpose. As time goes by, temples harbour fewer monks, and those who remain are less likely to talk to outsiders about Buddhism. A person who shows too much interest in meditation might find that it wasn't good for his or her 'social credit' algorithm. In the end, the building remains; the content fades away. It's not easy for modern Chinese to get in touch with their historical culture, even though the façade of old heritage stands magnificently around them.

In Thailand, tourist hordes tramp through Bangkok's Grand Palace, but the Temple of the Emerald Buddha is still a place of worship, and the throne rooms are there to seat a living king. It's still common for young men to spend some time as Buddhist monks, when they experience meditation and spiritual teachings first hand. Many children, at least in villages, learn how to cook, how to make flowers and how to dance. That said, the bond is weakening in Bangkok. For the kids with orange hair who cluster around Siam Square, the village may not be so far away, but the classical culture is another world. This would be true of youth everywhere, but the gap is sharper and more severe in Asia.

Until recently, aside from the loyal old ladies at the National Theatre, the largest group of people who went to see traditional dance were the foreigners in the audience at Sala Chalermkrung Royal Theatre and other tourist venues around the city. However, by the late 2000s, one could feel a new stirring within Bangkok.

Certain dance shows, such as the Royal Khon staged

in winter 2007 got a 'buzz,' and Queen Sirikit attended as a sign of the revival of royal patronage. In 2019, Khru Kai and Peeramon mounted a Khon performance at Thai Cultural Centre that drew thousands of enthusiastic Thais to the theatre. Khon has come back from the dead.

Meanwhile, Khru Kai is much in demand to take his dancers and puppeteers around the world. Living here in Bangkok, I sometimes don't see him for months, because he's off performing in Buenos Aires or Prague. Aside from its domestic impact, tourism builds a community of support around the world, and this engenders an appetite abroad for 'Things Thai'.

Dance and all the arts are evolving to reflect the taste of the new patrons. Once it was kings and courtiers who were the arbiters of elegance. Now, it's Korean and German tourists. Hence the popularity of all-in-one 'Thai culture' shows like Bangkok's lavish tourist extravaganza Siam Niramit. Like it or not, that's the way Bangkok is going.

The pluses and minuses of tourism make themselves felt in unexpected ways. In the design of restaurants and resorts Japan suffered because, not needing to appeal to foreign tastes, it failed to innovate and fell behind world standards. Thailand, inundated with foreign visitors, went the other way. The quantity of well-designed apartments and restaurants in Bangkok contrasts strongly with the plastic-and-fluorescent-light approach of Tokyo. In this respect, Thailand is the 'advanced' country, and Japan a 'developing nation'.

On the other hand, traditional arts in Japan benefited

by not having to pander to busloads of ignorant outsiders. Until recently, Japan escaped the tourist glitz we see at Siam Niramit. Kabuki and other forms of theatre had to think up ways to attract audiences within Japan, and in the process they stayed closer to their classic forms, while coming up with innovations that are truly original.

As I write, at the height of the Covid-19 pandemic of 2020–21, Bangkok is at a historic turning point. Tourism has screeched to a halt. In our lifetimes, none of us has ever seen a Bangkok like this, devoid of tourists. The hotels, shops, temples and palaces are empty, except for Thais and a few expact residents, some of whom are enjoying the new-found peace and quiet.

The question is what comes next. Tourism will recover, but it may be years before tourists return in anything like their former numbers. Japan enjoyed an inbound boom in the late 2010s and became economically dependent on tourism, so for Japan too the withdrawal pains are severe. But, unlike Thailand, Japan has never been *culturally* dependent on tourism.

In Thailand, and particularly in Bangkok, there's a question of where creative energies will now flow. Early signs are that artists, especially dancers and musicians, are turning to the internet, YouTube and so forth, to create their experimentations. The new forms that we're seeing are aimed inside the country, not outside.

As for the popular culture – pop songs, TV, the everyday ways in which restaurants and cars are decorated, fashions and so on – these depended less on the tourists and foreign residents, and so they will likely go on with the same verve as before. And yet these too had hardly developed in a vacuum, their rich variety emerging out of a bubbling fusion of Thai and foreign ingredients. With the spigot of foreign travellers turned off for the first time in close to eighty years, no one can guess what the impact on popular culture will be.

Taming the Chaos

The appeal of Bangkok has been its chaotic overlay of peoples and neighbourhoods. This is where much of the romance and mystery is to be found. Walk behind a skyscraper and you might find a *khlong* still lined with palm trees. In the older parts of town, decaying mansions survive hidden inside slums; you can round a corner and stumble upon a *yaan* (old neighbourhood) that has existed for a century.

Civic administrators, especially under military control, which has lasted for most of the 2010s and is ongoing as of 2021, are determined to brush up the city and make Bangkok into Singapore. Under the name of 'preservation', old neighbourhoods are being erased.

The most notable case was the destruction of the 'town behind the walls', a community of about 300 people living in ramshackle wooden houses behind Mahakan Fort, which had survived since the days of Rama III. In 2018, despite near-unanimous opposition from experts and historical groups, the city evicted the residents, bulldozed the old wooden buildings and uprooted giant trees. To build – a park. Fort Mahakan now stands as a gleaming monument to national glory, no longer surrounded by people and a living community. The *yaan* has become a lawn.

The old royal centre of town, Rattanakosin Island (bounded by the Chao Phraya River to the west and concentric canals to the east), contains the Grand Palace, historic *wats* and government ministries, as well as old shophouses and a mix of grand homes and slums along the river. Under the banner of cultural preservation, the 'Rattanakosin Island Plan' is cleaning up the area. Ministry buildings are emptied of government offices and their occupants sent to new headquarters elsewhere. Slums are removed, or hidden behind giant billboards. Discordant elements, for example Western-looking buildings that don't look classically 'Thai', are redesigned or repurposed. It's hoped to turn the wider streets of the old town into a 'Champs Elysées', a stylish promenade.

Sprucing up the old city raises knotty questions of how to handle scenery and heritage. In 2019, it was mandated that all new buildings in the area must be painted in a unified beige, with slate-grey roofs. In cities like Kyoto or Rome, which really did have a unified scheme of colours and materials, such a project would have cultural validity. In Bangkok, where there never was such a unity, the effect is to create an anodyne 'historic district' with no history.

If Bangkok's true character is chaos, then plans like these only serve to water down what was fun about the city. On the other hand, should old buildings with historic value just be allowed to rot away, while getting more encrusted with wires, bad paint jobs and unsightly signage? Chaos is a result of how cities were planned or built, not an aim in and of itself. Restored shophouses and refurbished old ministry buildings really do look better.

To state the choice in terms of extremes: should the city aim for beauty and order – or artificial history and loss of character? Hopefully Bangkok will find some middle ground, and luckily there are academics and non-profits who keep an eye on these things and fight against, or at least stall for a while, the construction schemes of the bureaucrats.

The scarier plans are the ones that go beyond beautification to sterilization. None is more controversial than the Chao Phraya Promenade, which aims to line the banks of the river with kilometres of concrete embankments and bicycle lanes. Opponents point out that the damage to the ecology of the river, old neighbourhoods along the way and historic properties, will be severe, and as a result the plan – stopped at times by the courts, and then restarted – keeps getting modified. With each proposal, the embankment is redesigned, sometimes narrower, sometimes wider. At present it's been downscaled from 14 kilometres to 7 kilometres. As the decision making is so opaque, nobody knows what will finally get built. One thing is sure: eventually the river will be concreted; the colourful chaos of the riverbanks will be tamed.

Blandness

The thing that Bangkok always stood for – exuberant, sensuous, variety – is changing. Old neighbourhoods demolished, the town centre near the river refurbished as a showpiece, street food removed from the streets and relegated to official locations, markets replaced by malls – these are the direction of a bland new Bangkok that is coming.

Meanwhile, in the arts, censorship and the pressures of official 'Thainess' weigh down on dance, music, painting and architecture. There was a time when *indie* and *inter* were the cutting-edge. Now, the *indie*-ness is less *indie*, as youth grow less funky and more stylish. Bangkok is becoming more moneyed, the venues sleeker.

Tourism has been another engine driving the 'blandification' of Bangkok. The bureaucrats' desire to 'clean up the act' is partly aimed at pleasing the tourists. Unruly trees get chopped, malodorous and unsightly markets and street stalls get removed, shophouses get repainted in regulation beige. The decline of the unruly and unexpected – this is the undertext behind much recent writing on Bangkok.

In this, of course, Bangkok is not alone, as 'blandification' is the direction of the world. Even New York, for all its excitement and colour, is seeing drastic changes as we enter into the 2020s. With rents rising, bookstores, grocers and pizzerias close their doors, leaving block after block of shuttered street fronts, while landlords await the arrival of new renters in the form of deep-pocketed big chains. Gentrification has swept away much of the life of old neighbourhoods. To some degree, then, the new bland Bangkok that's coming is part of an irreversible world trend.

That said, it will be harder to tame Bangkok than many other cities. The complex interweave of ethnicities, Chinese shophouses, slums, social strata, land ownership in various colours, wide highways emptying into tiny lanes, street stalls which still somehow find a place – the city is a nearly impassable thicket full of branches, thorns and creeping vines. All the bureaucrats can do is to hack away at the edges, building a lawn here and promenade there – all soon to be overgrown with new vendors and user communities.

It wasn't for nothing that Thai artists in the old days took as their theme the wild forest of Himmaphan, full of weird trees and bizarre cross-mated animals. In Bangkok, the haunted jungle of a chaotic city will live on for a while.

Neo-Bangkok

Tradition, modernism, tourism, experimentation, censorship, 'Thainess', 'blandification' – all these things are part of the mixed salad that is Bangkok. The arts of traditional Bangkok as we see them now are what you might call 'Neo-Bangkok' – not old and not completely new either, a pastiche of elements.

Bangkok culture has changed so much over the previous two centuries that trying to figure out its true form is impossible. From the beginning Thailand's rulers freely mixed Khmer, Chinese and Western motifs. In Bangkok's palaces, Gothic arches and Corinthian columns vie with carved *naga* serpents and *chofa* finials. In the process everything got mixed up, and the mixing continues.

Khon – try to find someone (besides Peeramon and Khru Kai) who can tell you what these things really are. There's the official explanation, and there's the reality of classical dance today, which is that nobody knows what to look for any more. Meanwhile, Khon, with a fresh and younger Thai audience, is going its own new way.

As for Thai puppets, they may have been influenced by Japan, but there's nothing Japanese about the seductive movements of Thai puppeteers, almost more riveting to watch than the puppets themselves. By now the two- or three-man puppeteer system has become Thai. Focusing on the Japanese source is futile.

It just doesn't matter, because, in the hands of Khru Kai, the puppeteers and Pichet, the Thais are doing what they've done for a millennium: taking their core culture and fusing it with new influences. In the process, no matter how 'Neo' it gets, they reproduce in a new form the elusive Thai qualities that have always been here.

Misty Landscape

ทิวทัศน์ในม่านหมอก

14

เขตจตุจักร

s a night person, I avoid early mornings at all costs. Yet in Bangkok, for
several years, I found myself leaping
out of bed with excitement every Friday morning at daybreak, concerned
only that others might have woken up before me. I was
on my way to Chatuchak Market for the dawn gathering
of pot collectors.

In the late 1990s, on Friday morning, the antique
dealers quietly opened for business. A weekly caravan
brought antiques down in trucks from the Burmese or
Cambodian borders, from holes in the ground around

Sukhothai and prehistoric sites in Isarn. In the early pre-dawn hours they unloaded parcels wrapped in newsprint and laid out dirt-encrusted pots in stalls located in discreet corners of the market. A gaggle of Bangkok's collectors were there, vying with each other to snatch the finest pieces as they came unwrapped.

By the time I arrived, the usual group had already gathered. There was Harold, who first introduced me to Chatuchak's Friday morning ritual, and beside him, smiling Mr Soong from River City antiques centre along the river. A little later, some rich Thai-Chinese buyers would arrive. There was a pecking order: the dealers offered Mr Soong the best pieces first. As he was the

Prehistoric Thai black earthenware pot with incised patterns, c.1000 BC.

biggest spender in the market, it was essential to keep him smiling.

Then came the rest of us, and after we'd taken our pick, the market continued on into the weekend, when the Bangkok day-trippers arrived, looking for trinkets. A week later, you would see the best pots on view at Mr Soong's shop in River City, gleaming behind glass show-windows for five or ten times the price.

I arrived in Bangkok in 1997 convinced that I knew quite a lot about the traditional culture of East Asia, only to find that the vast world of Southeast Asian art and history was a mystery to me. I embarked on a pro-cess of study, and my first teacher was Harold.

Harold is an Australian architect who came to Thai-land and discovered a side of himself that he never knew existed. One day in the mid-1990s, he was shown a black prehistoric Thai pot. It had a flared and fluted, strangely contemporary shape, carried striking zigzag patterns and, he was told, was 3,000 years old. Price: 500 baht. Harold was hooked and by the time I met him was several years into putting together a world-class collection of Thai ceramics.

Learning at Chatuchak Market

Inspired by Harold, I also wanted to make a collection, but my senses weren't trained. Harold and a lady dealer in Chatuchak named Mui took me in hand. She told me

Thai earthenware pot, *c*.1500 BC, recreated from broken shards.

to my delight that the little fifteenth-century incense box that I'd bought as a student from the street-market at Sanam Luang was a genuine piece. I also learned that this was pure good luck.

The first thing I learned at Chatuchak, and one of the first words I mastered in Thai, was *som*, which means 'repaired'. Most prehistoric pots are found in burial sites, and thousands of years of accumulated earth have crushed them into shards large and small. Finding a complete and undamaged pot is rare. The dealers take the shards and put them back together, like solving a jigsaw puzzle, gluing the pieces together, sometimes crudely with cement, and other times ingeniously with resin, painting the surface with perfectly matched acrylics.

When it comes to ceramics of later eras, such as sixteenth-century Sukhothai pots, resin and acrylic technique is truly exquisite, producing exactly the same textures and tones as ancient greenish-blue celadons. Only the most expert eye can see the difference, and I never acquired the skill. I relied on Mui, who would kindly show me where the repair was. Often, when I thought I had found the perfect Sukhothai bowl, Mui would turn it over in her hands, pronounce the dreaded word *som*, and I would learn that only the foot was original; all the rest was resin.

Outright fakes – of which no part is original – are also common, especially of Khmer vases, with their noble forms shaped like Roman amphoras. After weeks and months of attending the Friday vigils, I found that thoughts of pots burrowed inside and went unconscious – I'd have a revelation about a northern Thai jar while in the shower or at the supermarket. Not every revelation was a happy one.

At one point I fell in love with Vietnamese ceramics and splurged on two spectacular finds, a large plate and a blue-and-white jar, from a reputable London dealer. I displayed them at home as prized pieces until one day, when the afternoon sun fell at a certain angle, I noticed something odd about the glaze of the jar. It nagged at me for some months until finally I took some solvent to the jar, and, sure enough, the entire surface bled away, revealing a few faded shards embedded in a base of plain white clay. All the rest had been latex. I don't blame the dealer because he was probably fooled as well as I had been. But it was a cold reminder that there is no such thing as a reputable dealer. On the other hand, the plate was good. You never know.

Gradually I learned. Every Friday was like attending a seminar in some little-known branch of Southeast Asian ceramics. At one point hundreds of spouted seventh-century vessels in white and orange clay from southern Thailand filled the stalls, so many that one might have thought they were mass-produced fakes. But they were real, all unearthed from one site, and a few weeks later they were gone, never to be seen again.

Some years later the market was awash with eighteenth-century Vietnamese jars stuffed with bronze coins, fused together by seawater, which seemed to have come from a shipwreck. It was as if an ancient bank had gone down to the bottom of the ocean. These money pots too were like nothing anyone had seen before. Each collector in Bangkok got at least one, Mr Soong, of course, skimming off the best, and then the money pots disappeared.

Part of the fun of a place like Bangkok is that there's still so much lying undiscovered and unstudied. You can be a true adventurer. For example, the markets sometimes featured tall Lao water jars, similar to Khmer jars but with a pronounced lip and a glaze with brighter lustre. Some said they were sixteenth-century, others nineteenth-century. And there's the question of what's 'Lao'. When people say 'Lao', sometimes they mean the country that now is called 'Laos' and other times they're talking about the parts of northeast Thailand where Lao-speaking people live. Words like 'Lao', 'Khmer' and 'Thai' are artificial, since the boundaries of kingdoms and ethnic groups shifted over the centuries.

There's room here for someone to carve out a career as a 'Lao ceramics specialist' – so far, to my knowledge, there are none. This contrasts greatly with China and Japan, where every obscure glaze has a library of specialist books written about it.

People have been living in Thailand and its surroundings for a very long time. Thai prehistoric ceramics are among the world's oldest, and burial sites will continue to be found for hundreds of years to come. In prehistoric times, every village would have had an artisan firing vessels in a heap of burning rice husks; in Sukhothai and Ayutthaya, vast kilns supplied a ceramics business that exported all over Southeast Asia and as far away as Japan. At one point in the late sixteenth century it's believed that the ceramics exports of Thailand rivalled those of Ming China.

I once calculated that if 1,000 potters produced three pots per day, that would be about one million pieces per year. After 3,000 years, that's three billion pieces. If just one-tenth of one per cent survived, it means there are three million pieces of ceramic waiting to be discovered.

Beyond Ceramics
Of course, it's not just pots that flood into the Bangkok art market. Furniture from China and Tibet, wood and marble Buddhas from Myanmar, stone and bronze sculpture from Cambodia, have made Bangkok into one

of the world's leading art emporia. With big money at stake, fakery is a huge problem, and the artisans who forge Khmer sculpture have access to technologies far beyond painted resin. They mine stones from the original Khmer quarries near Mount Kulen, and they age their artefacts by coating them with cocktails of mud and chemicals. Above and beyond these techniques, a good counterfeiter must truly love Khmer art and have an instinct for what is beautiful. At this fuzzy boundary, fakery and great artistry merge.

As I was straining to absorb the arcane knowledge of pots and sculpture, I came face to face with a different kind of learning experience. It began early on, when I had borrowed some Khmer statues from a River City dealer to decorate my apartment. An old friend who worked for UNESCO came to visit one day and, taking one look at the stone torsos, he recoiled in horror. 'How could you lend your hand to the despoiling of Cambodia's national heritage?' he asked.

It came as a rude jolt because in all my years in Japan it had never entered any of our heads that art collecting could be anything but a good. Connoisseurship of the relics of the past was key to the cultured world of the Chinese and Japanese literati – it was through studying old bronzes and calligraphies that they refined their inner souls.

In Southeast Asia, it's in mute carved figures and the shapes of jars that the secrets of the ancients survive. A Khmer sculpture speaks worlds about the nobility of kingship. A Sukhothai *phan* stem-cup reveals an attitude to the divine. It's not enough to just see these things behind glass in museums, because, as the literati know, it's living with art works over time that slowly teaches us their lessons.

But what if these objects have been chopped from shrine façades, or smuggled out of archaeological sites before they could be studied and their provenance known? In wealthy Japan, the government and museums have a chance to purchase important objects before they leave the country, but this has not been true in poor Southeast Asian countries. During the Khmer Rouge regime and into the mid-1990s, the pillage that took place in Cambodia knew no bounds.

In one notorious case in the late 1990s, a Thai collector arranged to have an entire wall of the ancient city of Banteay Chhmar in northern Cambodia transferred to his residence. Using army cadets, they sawed the wall

Phan stem-cup: sixteenth-century Sukhothai celadon.

into hundreds of blocks, but the truck convoy was stopped as it entered Thailand. Only part of the wall was recovered, but later the Thai government returned what it had to the National Museum in Phnom Penh, where this portion of the reconstructed wall can be seen today.

Against this background of theft and knavery, art collecting – which was a benign form of self-improvement in Japan and China – took on a darker tone here in Bangkok. I returned the borrowed torsos to River City and began to think about what the limits might be.

There are those who say that no object should ever leave its country of origin. But this overlooks the fact that art objects transferred to other countries serve as 'cultural ambassadors'. Many a love affair with China began when a little boy or girl saw their first ceramics or paintings in a museum in France or Australia. Without this first-hand contact with the artefacts of other nations, our understanding of other cultures would be truly poverty-stricken.

At the same time, it seems right that the important pieces should remain in their countries of origin as cultural patrimony. It's a question of balance. Japan has a regime of rating art works which dates back a century by now. 'National Treasures' and 'Important Cultural Properties' can never be exported; everything else can be sent anywhere in the world. This system allows for a legitimate art market, while protecting the pieces that are treasures of the nation.

The problem in Southeast Asia is that there is no legitimate art market. Thailand, for example, prohibits

Thai earthenware pot, *c*.1500 BC,
recreated from broken shards.

by law the import and export of *all* Buddhist sculptures.
This blanket ban means that even the most innocent
trade in plastic Buddha replicas is illegal – there is no
distinction between a souvenir gewgaw and a rare Sukhothai bronze – hence chaos rules.

It seems a bit much to insist that every shard of
antique ceramic must stay in Thailand when there are
three million pots yet to be discovered. In the case of
Cambodian bronzes, tens of thousands, maybe hundreds of thousands, were created during the millennium
of the Khmer Empire. What the market needs is rules
that would differentiate between what's important and
what's less so.

A legalized art market brews a store of knowledge.

Dealers and collectors often know more than curators, who tend to get their knowledge second-hand and not on the ground. Only dealers came to Chatuchak's Friday mornings, which means that only the dealers had the true knowledge of where things came from.

There's a rule in the art world that architectural fragments are frowned upon because they despoil buildings in situ; and anything known to be stolen, or that has been previously published, is out of bounds. But if the statue is unknown and comes fresh out of the ground somewhere, it's considered fair game. This approach is questionable, since there is much to be learned about where and how a piece was found, and much knowledge is lost when smugglers yank a piece from the earth and ship it off to Bangkok. Nevertheless, at least a rule such as this draws some limits. It's the beginning of an organizing principle, which is what the art market here has lacked.

The End of Art Collecting
The knotty issues facing me in Bangkok made me think about what antique collectors and dealers really do. When it comes to Southeast Asia, plenty of skulduggery went on in the smuggling of antiques out of Cambodia and Myanmar. On the other hand, art collectors often are able to save pieces that would otherwise be lost or destroyed. This has especially been true in Asia, where

modernization has swept all before it and villagers think nothing of chopping up old houses for firewood, regilding or even reshaping bronze Buddhas so drastically as to efface all signs of the original, and leaving precious textiles to mice and rot while clothing themselves in T-shirts from Tesco.

Nor is this just the practice of villagers in the Southeast Asian countryside. The same is true of advanced Japan, where people continue to tear down grand houses that are hundreds of years old and throw away antique lacquer trays because these aren't 'modern' enough. In China and Tibet, where the state itself set out to destroy the past, treasures smuggled out to international museums are among the few that survive. Collectors and dealers snatch what they can from the jaws of the great compactor crunching up Asia's cultural heritage.

Private collections are part of what makes Bangkok a cultural capital. Of the foreign collectors, Jim Thompson is best known, with his small but choice collection of Thai antiques in his canal-side complex. Actually, the biggest buyers active in the antiques market have been Thai. Thai princes collected avidly in the early and mid-twentieth century, and their acquisitions form the base of our knowledge of Thai art today. Prince Chumbhot's collection, housed in the Suan Pakkard Palace, preserves among other things a priceless pavilion from Ayutthaya with early gold-lacquer painting. Another example of a private Thai museum is the Prasart Collection, housed in spacious grounds in the eastern suburbs of Bangkok.

The way the trend is going, collectors in the future will

have few chances to make such contributions. As happens in rarefied academic fields, extreme ideologies take hold. There's a vocal group among non-profits and academia who disapprove of *all* collecting, even crafts from villages. It 'disturbs the community'. Hopefully the community will keep producing their crafts – even if there are no outside buyers. But if not, nobody should interfere.

From moral disapproval, the next step is the Inquisition. In America, in the spring of 2008, the IRS investigated dealers in California who were allegedly helping their clients to donate Thai prehistoric pots to museums at inflated prices for tax write-offs. Zealous agents carried out highly publicized raids of major art institutions such as Los Angeles County Museum. Overnight, Thai prehistoric pottery everywhere came under a cloud, even though its import into America was not illegal. Finally, agents arrested Roxanna Brown, a friend of mine and director of the Ceramics Museum in Bangkok, who had returned briefly to Seattle to give a talk. They must have believed that they had finally caught a really big fish. However, frail Roxanna was neither a dealer nor a collector; she was a meek 'pure scholar'. Caught in the net, she couldn't stand the shock and she died in prison.

Raids of major museums, a colleague arrested and dead in jail – the nitty-gritty of Thai art was worlds away from the uplifting realm of the Chinese literati which I had idealized. Following the Roxanna Brown scandal, the authorities started to quietly crack down on the prehistoric antiques trade in Thailand. It happened over a number of years, but imperceptibly the weekly flow into

Chatuchak slowly dried up, and by the early 2010s, most of the stalls had disappeared. The Friday-morning sessions were held no longer.

Out of My Hands

Although I stopped collecting, I was pleased at having been able to acquire the pots that I picked up at Chatuchak, especially when I realized that the chance was gone, maybe forever, for anyone to collect in this way. Meanwhile, something else happened. It's now over twenty years since I made my 'return' to Bangkok in 1997, and in the meantime – I got older.

No longer of an age to be buying more art, I started thinking about who should own those prehistoric pots. In 2019, I donated the whole lot to the Cultural Ministry of Thailand. They're no longer mine; they belong to the nation. One thing I tried to do was to pass on the knowledge from Chatuchak and so with every piece I supplied a note with whatever bits of information I'd gleaned from Mui and the other shopkeepers in those pre-dawn hours.

I'm happy to have once owned pieces that were truly wondrous. I was lucky to be in the last generation that would hold these things in our hands and absorb through our fingers their secrets of earth and fire. They're in museum cases and behind glass now – or more likely, sitting in boxes in the basement – but in any case, they now

Prehistoric Thai black earthenware pot with incised patterns, *c.*500 BC.

belong to the world of the curators. Having given them away, I find that I don't need any more to own things like this.

While antiques are no longer as rich a collecting field in Thailand as they used to be, traditional craft does still thrive in Thailand. Thanks to the tourists, you can hardly walk more than ten feet in Bangkok without seeing it. Much of it is mass-produced souvenir *chachkas*, but the tourist trade is also sparking a design renaissance that is making Bangkok into the design hub of Southeast Asia.

Which brings us full circle to Chatuchak. Antiques actually make up only a tiny fraction of the market, which features everything from puppies to teak houses, but it's especially rich in traditional crafts and new Thai design.

An example of this is Thai blue-and-white ceramics done in a repetitive design called *lai taa sapparot* ('eye of pineapple pattern') With its scalloped outline brushed in loops of indigo blue, finished off with a line and a dot in the middle, the pattern is easy to draw and so can be made cheaply in great quantity. Mass produced – yet even now mostly drawn by hand – it has become a typical form of Thai daily ware, and at Chatuchak you find stalls selling it in every format, plates, bowls, flower jars and more.

While now seen as traditionally Thai, 'eye of pineapple' is in fact something new. It seems to have come into vogue some time after the 1960s. Like many of the small things of Thai life, no one seems to have studied it, so there's no way to know how it originated. My guess is that artisans working at the same mom-and-pop kilnsites

Chatuchak design: modern blue-and-white daily
ware with 'eye of pineapple' design

271

that made *benjarong* adapted Chinese brushwork to *Lai Thai* design.

In *benjarong* plates, they would draw intricate circular patterns expanding outwards like a net, which they laboriously traced in hundreds of tiny lines. But when it came to making cheaper blue-and-white ware, they dipped a Chinese brush in cobalt-blue glaze and daubed loose crescent outlines on a white base. Thus a new design product was born.

'Eye of pineapple' dishes are so commonplace that they go practically unnoticed by writers on Thai design. And yet, they're a classic Thai fusion. A simple airy pattern like this never existed anywhere else. It's the same playful line that so impressed Harold when he saw these zigzags on his first prehistoric pot.

My relationship with Thai antique art did not turn out the way I thought it would in 1997. There's a story about a Chinese literatus who sees in his youth a precious painting of a misty mountain landscape So struck is he by the painting with its towering cliffs and wisps of cloud that he spends the rest of his life trying to find it again. But when he finally tracks the scroll down, he's disappointed. What if the painting he saw so long ago was not really the masterpiece he imagined it to be, or even a fake? And then he realizes that it doesn't matter because the misty landscape is engraved in his heart; he has absorbed its essence and so he has no need for the real painting itself.

Expats

ฝรั่งอพยพ

15

เขตต่างดาว

I n Japan I had few foreign friends. The very word 'expat' was unfamiliar. Expats were stockbrokers in Tokyo, not me. Everything changed when I moved to Bangkok, where I was an outsider, barely able to cope in Thai, and unfamiliar with Thai ways. In Bangkok I discovered a vibrant expat community, and they became my friends.

Being a writer, I gravitated to other writers. Thailand supports a strong community of journalists and creative writers because for decades it has been the hub for reporters on Southeast Asia. Many of the leading photographers and correspondents of East Asia make Bangkok their home.

One friend whom I met early on was British journalist Philip Cornwel-Smith, with whom I shared many epiphanies about Thailand and Bangkok. Philip has focused on Thai popular culture. He researched and photographed the details of Bangkok's ongoing fusion, from the neon lights of temple festivals to decorated tuktuks. I ended up editing his books and in the process followed Philip on his journey into the small things of daily life that other writers had overlooked.

The world's appetite for titillating writing on Bangkok has been good for novelists, who thrive on the city's reputation for sex and drugs. Several friends of mine have written Bangkok novels – in fact the 'Bangkok novel' has become a genre unto its own. Like everyone else, I also have an idea for a Bangkok novel. But sadly, John Burdett, author of *Bangkok 8* and its sequels, has already beaten us all to worldwide fame with his intricately scripted thrillers, centred on Soi Cowboy.

The most literary of the Bangkok novelists is Canadian Christopher Moore, who lives just down the street from me. His earlier novel series was the 'Land of Smiles': *A Killing Smile*, *A Haunting Smile* and more *Smiles*. In recent years, with his grittier *Vincent Calvino* mysteries culminating with the futuristic *Dance to the End of Time*, he's created a 'Bangkok Noir' world in which we discover, as Gore Vidal said of these novels, 'the razor teeth behind the Smile'.

Bangkok murder mysteries: *Bangkok 8* by John Burdett (2003) and *Dance to the End of Time* by Christopher G. Moore (2020).

The Orchid Club

I noticed that there was a contrast between how expat journalists wrote about their adopted country. In Japan, foreigners often undergo a 'conversion experience', after which they build careers celebrating everything Japanese: the bureaucrats are elite, the artists live on a higher moral plane and so on. This group of writers has even earned a name: the 'Chrysanthemum Club'.

In Thailand, in contrast, there doesn't appear to be an 'Orchid Club'. Thailand-specialists are well aware of the country's problems, and their writings tend to be sharp. The closest thing to the Chrysanthemum Club type of literature would be the gushing squibs that appear in tourist magazines.

There's quite a market for effusive travel writing, and plenty of people make their living from it. However, what doesn't exist is the really big money that pours into think tanks and university chairs funded by Japanese government and businesses. That's what makes favourable writing about Japan a stepping-stone to success. Thailand doesn't offer the same carrots to foreign journalists and academics.

Another factor is Japan's twentieth-century success story. Foreigners come to Japan impressed with the fact that, as an Asian nation, it rose to compete on equal terms with the West. For many, that leads them to believe that Japan is a promised land, a place that does everything differently, and yet with success. Thailand, still relatively poor, fills few with the romance of 'Asian success'. So people start right out by looking at Thailand with a critical eye.

The writers, of course, make up only a fraction of the expatriate community. It includes businessmen who've come here to seek their fortunes. Many a Frenchman or Italian owns his own restaurant, which is why the French and Italian food here is better than almost anywhere else in Asia. Others have built middle-to-large companies in real estate, construction, hotels and PR.

Until recently, it has been easy to live here for years, even without a proper visa. Thailand gave us time. Young people with no plan in mind came to Bangkok, bounced around for a bit and then found something to do, often something they never could have imagined. Harold, collector of antique Thai ceramics, worked as an architect for years before he discovered an interest in prehistoric pots. This is how the expats 'recreate' themselves. Today, the city harbours the largest and most thriving expat population in this part of the world.

Not every foreigner here aspires to make a splash like Jim Thompson, who revived the silk industry in the 1950s and left behind an arts foundation that continues to make an impact on the city. More reclusive types prefer to live quietly among their books and gardens, rather in the style of Daoist scholar John Blofeld. My cousin Tom likes nothing more than to come home to the green oasis of his Ladphrao house after a day at the office and settle in with a recording of classical music and a good book. Bangkok is a good place to submerge and devote oneself to one's hobbies, or vices. Life is inexpensive, and the neighbours do not much intrude.

The most numerous kind of foreigner is, of course, not the resident, but the tourist. They come and go, many in the process falling in love with a boyfriend or a girlfriend. And they are legion. When I lived in Indra Condominium in Pratunam, it seemed that every other apartment was leased to a Thai supported by a lover abroad. The foreign patrons travel to Thailand for a few months and spend the rest of the year back in their home countries, where they have jobs and spouses. Many choose Thailand in the end, but the transition can take decades. The number of foreigners who live partly in Bangkok, partly somewhere else must be many tens of thousands.

The 'friends and lovers' group has its soft underbelly, the ageing philanderers who troll the depths of Bangkok's go-go bars. For them, Bangkok is an addiction. It's the sight of a fat elderly Westerner walking hand-in-hand down the street with a comely young Thai woman that draws the disapproving stare of many a tourist. Disreputable though they may be, this group too adds to the spice of the city. It's expats like these that make Bangkok truly exotic.

For the philanderer the fun ends all too soon, when a Thai woman or man snares him. To support spouse and family, pretty soon he's running a business or forging a career like the rest of us. Patrick Gauvain, the American photographer known by the name of 'Shrimp', exemplifies 'The Rake's Progress'. A photographer who lived in Bangkok for decades, Shrimp was known for his annual calendar of Asian female nudes. Now married and well established, he still describes himself, a bit wistfully, as 'an old reprobate'. At the far end of the expat spectrum, a handful of foreigners have mastered Thai language and become Thai citizens. This, while more common for Chinese and Indians, is unusual for a Westerner and has become vanishingly rare today.

Absorbing the *Farang*

By 'expat society', I speak of Westerners. Thais are so diverse that other Asians such as Chinese and Japanese can more easily blend in. Westerners, however, will always stand out. My cousin Tasi, when she worked as a volunteer at the Khlong Toei slum, was bemused at the way the schoolchildren gathered around her, asking for her autograph and giggling at her. It was her blonde hair, her pale white skin and, from a Thai perspective, her ample proportions

We *farang* differ in physique strongly, sometimes even drastically, from the populations within which we dwell in East Asia. As George Kates pointed out from his experience in Beijing in the 1930s, we have knock-knees, big noses and blotchy complexions; we tend to be tall and fat; we bump into things. As they say in Italy, we're 'a hair in the soup'. It's something I grew up with in Japan, so I've come to take it for granted.

M. R. Chakrarot remarks, 'In the Traiphum cosmology, there are Arabs to the west, and Chinese to the east. To the north are a race of crazy people so advanced that they don't need to work. They live to be 900 years old, and if they need something, they simply go to a magical tree and wish on it. I think it's an old lampoon on you Europeans.'

Given the strangeness of this tribe from the north, it's all the more remarkable that Thailand handles the *farang* with such aplomb. This is the most welcoming country for a Westerner in Asia. The number of intermarriages must be huge. I've seen TV specials about villages in Isarn that consist almost exclusively of Thai women married to foreigners, with the lanes full of mixed-blood children.

In Bangkok, the offspring of Thai-Western marriages, known as *luk-khrueng* ('half children'), or *luk-siew* ('crescent children', for those with only a quarter or less of foreign blood), have a position which has been denied to such people in China or Japan. Here, they dazzle as stars of Thai soaps because of their unusual appearance, and with often superior education they serve as managers in large corporations. One *luk-siew*, Bird McIntyre, dominated pop music for decades as Thailand's biggest pop-star.

The mixture of races has been going on a long time, with Westerners playing a role ever since the early 1600s, when the Dutch, British and traders sailed up-river to the old royal capital of Ayutthaya. The nineteenth century saw a fresh wave of Western adventurers, and from that time on they've kept coming. It's no wonder that Thailand by now would be used to mixed races, but from the perspective of other Asian nations, acceptance of the *luk-khrueng* is the greatest evidence of Thailand's open-mindedness.

The all-time most famous resident must be Anna Leonowens of *Anna and the King of Siam*, brought to Bangkok to tutor King Rama IV's children in English in the 1860s. She was hardly as close to him as her memoirs make out, but King Rama IV did have close foreign friends and advisors who visited him regularly in the palace, and to whom he wrote letters in English.

Siam's capital flourished as polyglot crossroads long

before Anna, or even the founding of Bangkok. Royal Ayutthaya during the seventeenth century gained its wealth through trade, becoming international in a way that was unique in Far East Asia. The city hosted communities of Dutch, British, French, Portuguese, Chinese, Persians, Japanese and Macassars from the island of Celebes. King Narai's favourite dinner was Persian, his desserts were Japanese.

King Narai sent embassies to Louis XIV in Versailles and imported mirrored glass from France to decorate his palaces. His chief minister was a Greek adventurer named Constantine Phaulkon. A family of Persian extraction known as the Bunnags helped manage palace finances, surviving centuries of ups and downs to serve in high positions at court until the early twentieth century. While no longer viceroys and ministers, Bunnags still hold a high place in Bangkok society today.

Phaulkon's rise and fall offers a useful lesson. Shipping out as a cabin boy from a stony island in the Adriatic, Phaulkon made his way to Thailand, where he took a job with the British East India Company. With fluent Thai, he caught the eye of King Narai, who elevated him in the 1680s to the post of a powerful minister. His heyday didn't last long. Disturbed at Phaulkon's and the French's undue influence, in 1688, the courtier Phra Petracha carried out a palace revolution that overthrew all of the King's relatives and palace guard. He ordered Phaulcon executed, and, after becoming king, Phra Petracha threw the French out of Thailand and had their bibles and crucifixes gathered up and burned.

Constantine Phaulkon (1685) attending (bottom left) at King Narai's
audience with French ambassadors.

While the doors were not shut as tightly as Japan's, Thailand remained closed to Westerners until the early nineteenth century. Phra Petracha's revolution has appeared to be a setback, the end of a golden age in which King Narai welcomed people from all over the globe to a cosmopolitan capital. But it could be that Phra Petracha acted in the nick of time. These were the years when the Dutch and Spanish were gobbling up Indonesia and the Philippines; the British and the French were soon to vie over India. Western colonization – done in the name of bringing Christian salvation to the natives – was about to sweep over Asia, and Phaulkon was the opening gambit. One could argue that Phra Petracha saved Siam.

The moral of the story is that outsiders are to be welcomed so long as they don't destabilize society. Within Thailand, there was a backlash against the Chinese in the 1920s, and another anti-Chinese period lasting from the end of the Second World War until the 1970s.

In recent years, Thailand's government has started to wrestle with the problem of undesirable Westerners. After a series of scandals in the early 2000s, the government announced rules that make it harder for foreigners to live here without work permits. As a result, there will be fewer who can take the time to simply hang around and discover themselves. The great era of Bangkok expats may have passed its zenith.

But we have left our mark on the city. There are hallowed halls within Bangkok that tourists rarely see but which cater almost exclusively to foreigners, such as the FCCT (Foreign Correspondents Club of Thailand). The venerable Siam Society, housed in leafy grounds on Soi Asoke just a block from where I live, hosts talks and events, and maintains a well-stocked research library.

One of the most active volunteer societies is the National Museum Volunteers (NMV), a society mainly of foreign women. These are docents, offering their services as guides at the National Museum, but they also sponsor seminars and study tours. With a history dating back decades, and dozens of members, the 'NMV' is a force to be reckoned with.

A Civilized Breakfast

Thailand learned its smooth treatment of foreigners in the nineteenth century. With the British moving in from the west and south, and the French from the east, Thailand needed to prove to the Westerners that it was 'civilized'. As dramatized in *The King and I*, it involved women wearing bustles and members of the court sitting down to formal dinner tables and eating with spoon and fork. Dan Beach Bradley, an Englishman living in Bangkok from the 1830s to the 1870s, who founded Bangkok's first newspaper, the *Bangkok Recorder*, describes an occasion when King Rama IV summoned him to the palace for breakfast. Except that only Beach was to eat. The King and his court sat watching him to see how he used the cutlery.

A similar process took place in Japan. In the 1870s they built a dance hall in Tokyo known as Rokumeikan ('Deer Cry Pavilion'), where society leaders practised waltz and minuet. All the court had to forgo kimono, and Western dress became an Imperial Family tradition: after his coronation, Emperor Hirohito was never seen again in Japanese costume, and the other male royals largely eschew kimono to this day.

Thailand's great modernizer King Rama V travelled to Europe in 1897 and returned with a taste for suits and cravats, cigars and liqueur. Shopkeepers still revere his image by offering on his altar a glass of tinted water in honour of the King's taste for brandy.

The rallying cry of the Western colonizers was that they were 'bringing civilization to the savage races of

๏หนังสือจดหมายเหตุฯ

THE BANGKOK RECORDER.

V.o.II เล่ม ๑ บางกอก เดือน หก ขึ้นเจ็ดค่ำ จุลศักราช ๑๒๒๗ March 1st 1865. คริศศักราช ๑๘๖๕ ใบ ๑ No. 1.

หนังสือ หลวง

๏ ชื่อ วัด, ชื่อ บ้าน, ชื่อ เมือง, ที่ มี อยู่ใน แผ่น ดิน ไทย. าง แห่ง ก็ เปน คำ ไทย แท้, ลาง แห่ง ก็ เปน คำ สังสกฤฎ แท้, างแห่ง ก็ เปน คำ เขมร. ก็ คำ ราษฎร เรียก ทั่ว ไป นั้น, มัก ยก ตาม คำ คน มาก, แล สั้น ๆ ง่าย ๆ. แต่ใน ราชการ คือ นังสือ ท้อง บัด ใบ ตรา มัก เรียก ยาว ๆ. แล เปน คำ สังสกฤฎ ไทย มาก. ถึง คำ สังสกฤฎ ก็ เรียก เตม. ฝ่าย ราษฎร แม้น เค่า สังสกฤฎ, ก็ เรียก ผิก ๆ ไป. ฯะ

๏ เมือง หนึ่ง มี ชื่อ สอง อย่าง สาม อย่าง, ฤๅ วัด หนึ่ง มี ชื่อ สอง อย่าง สาม อย่าง, ตาม คำ หลวง แล คำ ราษฎร, แล คำ เก่า คำ ใหม่, เมือง ที่ เปน เมือง หลวง เมือง ไทย บัด นี้, แต่ เดิม เปน หัว เมือง ชื่อ ธนบุรี, เปน ภาษา สังสกฤฎ. เขียน ตาม ครู ที่ เขา แปลง สังสกฤฎ เปน นังสือ โรม ดั่ง นี้. Dhanapuri. จะ เขียน อย่าง สอง ไทย อ่าน ไม่ ได้. แต่ คำ นี้ ใช้ ใน หนังสือ ราชการ, แต่ คำ ตลาด เรียก เมือง บางกอก ทั้ง นั้น, ฤๅ ลาง คำ เรียก สั้น ๆ, ว่า เมือง ธน, คู่ กับ เมือง นน. ก็ เมือง นน นั้น. ตาม ราชการ เรียก ว่า นันทบุรี, เขียน เปน สังสกฤฎ อย่าง ที่ ครู เขา แปลง เปน หนังสือ โรม, เขา เขียน ดั่ง นี้, Nandapuri. แต่ ใน หนังสือ ยาว เขียน ศรีมหาสมุท ต่อ ท้าย เข้า ทั้ง สอง เมือง. ศรี มหาสมุท เขียน ตาม สังสกฤฎ, ตาม ครู ที่ เขา แปลง เปน หนังสือ โรม, เขา เขียน ดั่ง นี้, Sri Maha Samudh แต่ คำ คน ทั้ง บ้าน ทั้ง เมือง, เมือง นน ก็ เรียก ว่า ตลาด ขวัน, เมือง ธน ก็ เรียก ว่า บางกอก. ต่อ ผู้ ดี ขึ้น มา น้อย, จึ่ง เรียก ว่า เมือง นน เมือง ธน. ที่ เรียก เตม, เขียน เตม. คำ สังสกฤฎ อย่าง ว่า นั้น, มี แต่ คำ กราบทูล ใน หลวง อย่าง หนึ่ง, เขียน ใน ท้อง บัด ใบ ตรา อย่าง หนึ่ง, คำ เรียก ไม่ ใคร่ มี. ฯะ

๏ ก็ ที่ เรียก บางกอก นั้น, คือ แต่ เดิม ลำ น้ำ ใหญ่, แต่ วัง น่า ลง มา จน ถึง วัง กรมหลวง วงษา ไม่ มี, เปน แผ่น ดิน. แม่ น้ำ เข้า ไป ตรง น่า วัง น่า, แล้ว ไป เลี้ยว ลง วัด ชี้ เหลก ตลิ่ง ชัน, แล้ว เลี้ยว มา ถึง บ้อม วัง กรมหลวง วงษา. เรือ กะเชียง เรือ แจว มา แต่ วัง น่า, ถึง วัง กรมหลวง วงษา, ทาง แต่ เช้า จน เยน, เวลา เช้า หุง เข้า อยู่ น่า วัง น่า ลืม ม่อ ไห ไว้, ล่อง เรือ มา ถึง น่า วัง กรมหลวง วงษา, จะ หุง เข้า เยน กิน, นึก ได้ ว่า ลืม ม่อ ไว้, จอด เรือ เข้า เดิน ยก ไป, เอา ม่อ มา หุง เข้า เยน กิน ทัน ได้. ที่ ริม บ้อม วัง กรมหลวง วงษา นั้น, มี คลอง หนึ่ง ปาก คลอง เข้า ไป ข้าง เหนือ, แล้ว คด เคี้ยว ไป ใน สวน วน เวียน อยู่, แล้ว ปลาย คลอง ไป ทะลุ ออก ที่ น่า วัง หลัง. ก็ ปาก คลอง ข้าง ล่าง นั้น ชื่อ บางกอก ใหญ่, ข้าง บน ชื่อ บางกอก น้อย. บาง นั้น แปล ว่า คลอง, คลอง บน กับ คลอง ล่าง เรียก บางกอก เหมือน กัน. ถ้า จะ เปรียบ เดี๋ยว นี้, เหมือน กับ ปาก ลัด แล บาง กรวย, ปาก ลัด ก็ เรียก ว่า ปาก ลัด บน, ปาก ลัด ล่าง. ที่ บาง กรวย นั้น ปาก ที่ ออก แม่ น้ำ ใหญ่ เรียก บาง กรวย นอก, ปาก ที่ ออก แม่ น้ำ น้อย เรียก บาง กรวย ใน. ถึง ปาก เตรจ ก็ เหมือน กัน นั้น ฉัน ใด, บางกอก น้อย บางกอก ใหญ่ ก็ เปน เช่น นั้น. แต่ ลำ แม่ น้ำ นั้น อ้อม ไป. ฯะ

๏ ก็ เมื่อ แผ่น ดิน พระเจ้า มหาจักรพรรดิ์, โปรด ให้ ขุด บาง กอก ใหญ่ บาง กอก น้อย, ให้ ทลุ ถึง กัน เปน แม่ น้ำ, แล้ว สร้าง เมือง ลง รักษา ที่ ขุด ลัด, เหมือน อย่าง แผ่นดิน พระบาท สมเดจ์ พระพุทธ เลิศหล้า นภาไลย, สร้าง เมือง นคร เขื่อนขันธ์, เขียน เปน สังสกฤฎ แต่ Nagar แต่ เขื่อนขันธ์ นั้น เปน คำ ไทย, จะ เขียน เปน คำ ไทย ก็ ได้. ที่ เดี๋ยว นี้ เรียก ว่า เมือง ปากลัด นั้น.

๏ ครั้น สร้าง เมือง ลง ที่ บางกอก ขุด ลัด แล้ว นั้น, ตั้ง ชื่อ ว่า เมือง ธนบุรี. การ ที่ ขุด อย่าง นี้ ถึง นาน กว่า สาม ร้อย ปี มา แล้ว ดู ก็ เหน จริง ดอก, ด้วย ลำ น้ำ ก็ ยัง แคบ กว่า ข้าง บน ข้าง ล่าง ไม่ ใช่ ฤๅ, กว้าง เพียง สี่ เส้น เสศ ไม่ ถึง ห้า เส้น. ครั้น ทาง ลัด มี ขึ้น แล้ว, น้ำ ลง เสีย ทาง ลัด, แม่ น้ำ เก่า ก็ แห้ง ไป

The Bangkok Recorder, 1865

the East'. Proud China and Burma would never bow to this pressure. The idea of taking pains to learn from the barbarian Westerners, as King Rama IV did with Dan Beach Bradley, was anathema. And so the Europeans overran them. However, Japan and Thailand did what was necessary. The fact that Japanese women wore lacy dresses and carried parasols, and the Thai King drank brandy, saved them. It proved that they were 'civilized'. It's a weird twist of history, but whether you got conquered or not had a lot to do with table manners.

Of course, much of the change was just on the surface. King Rama VI, who was educated at Sandhurst and Oxford, would seem to be the epitome of the English gentleman. He gave seated dinners at long tables spread with white linen, at which everyone wore bow ties and tails. Under the table, royal pages massaged the King's weary legs.

Both Japan and Thailand made the 'above the table' changes needed to keep the foreigners at bay, while keeping their old internal systems intact 'below the table'. The outside modernized, but the inside kept to its old ways.

In Thailand, the idea that 'Western is more civilized' explains why you will only rarely see people wearing traditional dress or living in an old-style house. For those of us Westerners who regret the way that East Asians seem so willing to cast aside their traditional culture in favour of things modern and Western, we should not forget that it was our own ancestors who set this train of events in motion. The Europeans arrived in their gunboats and delivered a shock that still reverberates, centuries later.

Thailand and Japan handled the foreigners similarly in the nineteenth century. But Japan's approach, once the nation stood well on its feet, was to get rid of them. Even now, only a tiny percentage of expats ever manage to set up their own businesses. Until very recently, most

Japanese saw few foreigners in their lives – although this has started to change with a big inbound tourism boom in the late 2010s. Yet despite much talk of 'internationalization', Japan's answer in the twenty-first century, as it was in the 1620s, has basically been to stay closed.

Farang Fatigue

Thailand, even during the fascist years before the Second World War, didn't have the option of keeping the foreigners out. Situated between British India and French Indochina, Thailand took the same approach that mercantile Ayutthaya had taken: welcome in the foreigners and profit from them.

Affections shift rapidly with political winds. In the late 1930s and early 1940s, Phibul Songkhram and the military dictatorship of the time saw the rising star of Japan and concluded they had no choice but to collaborate with the Imperial Army. When Japan did invade in December 1941, Thailand put up only a minimal resistance, choosing to work with the stronger party rather than fight them.

This was reversed in the later years of the war, when it became clear that Japan was going to lose. The Free Thai Movement, a splinter group who had resisted Japan from the beginning, now took over the government, Phibul Songkhram (for a few years) was removed from his position, and from there on Thailand fought the Japanese – in the process winning good treatment from the Allies at the conclusion of the war.

After the Second World War, a steady influx of Westerners established businesses or made careers as writers. With the Vietnam War in the 1960s and 1970s, floods of American military arrived, leaving the legacy of red light districts at Patpong in Bangkok, and at Pattaya, a weekend resort on the eastern seaboard. Today Pattaya forms the nexus of a huge expat retirement community, with apartments, restaurants and hospitals catering to foreign residents. In the 2000s came the Russians, who built a large and growing community. A decade later came a wave of Chinese.

From the 1980s, Thailand established itself as one of the world's premier tourist destinations. The backpackers swept in and built Khaosan Road into the youth mecca that it is today.

Meanwhile, Japanese companies invested heavily in Thailand, bringing in thousands of employees, followed by tens of thousands more working in Japanese restaurants, bars, even tatami-makers. In the 1990s, high-end package tourists from Europe and America spurred the growth of luxury resorts and spas. At my local Foodland supermarket I can buy newspapers not only in English but in French, German, Russian, Chinese, Japanese and Italian.

The juggling act goes on. In the 1970s and 1980s, Thailand built cosy relations with America; in the 1990s we heard much about 'Japan-Thailand friendship'. In the 2000s, it was China's turn, with ministers and diplomats attending Chinese festivals with great fanfare. As it has done for centuries, Thailand is balancing the ambitions of foreign powers while maintaining its freedom – and making money in the process.

As one might expect, there's another side to the welcome we Westerners receive in this country. After a warm encounter, the Thai goes home to his Thai universe, and the foreigner returns to an expat enclave.

There's something that I call '*farang* fatigue'. I've seen this happen in both Japan and Thailand. The young Japanese or Thai finds Westerners utterly exciting. He or she can't spend enough time with their Western friends, who seem to breathe the air of freedom, and from whom they sop up many an exhilarating idea about the world. Then, one day, the young Asian loses interest. He reverts to his own society, and his days of consorting with foreigners are over.

It's like when you go out for a drive on a nice sunny day. Your car is whizzing up into the hills, the sun is shining, the birds are chirping, and all is delightful. Then it's getting dark. You're far off in the mountains and you don't know where you are. From that moment onwards, you have only one thought in your mind: how to get home.

'Home' is the attitudes of reserve, the willingness to let vague things be, that form the basis of old East Asian societies. Our Western-style sharp and aggressive thinking will always act as a pressure on the Thais, and as a foreign resident here it's only prudent to keep in mind the effect that one might be having. '*Beua farang* [I'm sick of *farang*],' says my trusty assistant Saa. This from a woman who speaks fluent English, whose best friends have been Americans and who travels constantly to Europe. While I feel for the moment that this doesn't include me, it's a sign to be careful. It's time to guard against one's normal exuberance and practise a bit of reserve. But then, it was always time to do that.

Of course the fatigue goes both ways. The American poet Ezra Pound, long an expat in Italy, wrote, 'I am homesick after mine own kind/ Oh I know that there are folk about me, friendly faces / But I am homesick after mine old kind.' That's our plaintive chant, the song of the expats, who, wherever we are in the world, tend naturally to seek 'our own kind'.

The Role of Expats

Keeping the foreigners quietly in their place – this is how Thailand protects itself. For all their expert table manners that impressed ambassadors of the nineteenth-century powers, King Rama IV's and King Rama V's courts remained medieval autocracies. Thailand has mastered the art of accepting the external world and yet remaining itself. In this respect Thailand resembles Italy, another smiling 'la dolce vita' land, which has long been flooded with foreign visitors and even conquerors. Italy charms outsiders but keeps them at arm's length.

At the annual Oxford and Cambridge Dinner in Bangkok, one can see the end result of the 'civilizing' process that began with King Rama IV's English letters. Since Prince Svasti, Ping's ancestor, first went to study at Oxford in the nineteenth century, the sons and daughters of the upper class and the nobility have been going for generations to Oxford and Cambridge, and today they include bank presidents, prime ministers, college professors. If you gave the same party in Tokyo, few would hold any position of importance. Most would be unworldly second-tier academics. Here, they're society leaders who run the country.

At the Oxbridge Dinner, suave and worldly Thais give speeches sparkling with British wit that an American such as myself can hardly keep up with. Thailand, at least at this rarefied level, has truly mastered the Westerners' idiom. Although we're welcome here, the Thais have already got it all themselves. They just don't need us.

No Asian nation ever did. Seen from that point of view,

Oxbridge Dinner, December 2018: foreign residents with composer Somtow Sucharitkul, his parents, and former Prime Minister Anand Panyarachun.

the Thais are awfully nice about it. There is no question but that in Bangkok, for a foreigner, the ease of living and cordiality extended by the locals is far above any other Asian capital. Whether Thais are enjoying the encounter, or whether inside they are thinking, '*Beua farang*,' it makes little difference to the smiling welcome we receive.

But maybe Asian cities do need foreigners after all. Huge populations of expats make Paris, London and New York 'buzz' in a way that Tokyo never quite does. Expats are the yeast that makes the bread rise.

For a long time, Tokyo tried so hard to be 'international', but the role of foreigners was just too small to make a difference. However, from the later 2010s, Tokyo started to change with the arrival of a new generation of foreign entrepreneurs and internet influencers, and with them Tokyo's impact on the world is growing fast.

In contrast, in China, the number of foreigners is minimal, and as the net of surveillance tightens around them and their Chinese friends, they live in an ever more restricted circle. As a result, the impact of foreigners based in China is close to zero. Without that 'buzz', Beijing and Shanghai are having less and less to say to contemporary culture in the rest of the world.

Bangkok is at the other end of the spectrum. After a trip back to Japan, and especially after an excursion to China, returning to Bangkok feels like returning to where the action is. It's like that feeling you get when you come over the Hudson River and see the towers of Manhattan looming beyond the bridge.

It's nice to see our expat band as a kind of yeast. That, of course, doesn't change our fundamental irrelevance to Thai society. I'm grateful for good expat friends such as Philip Cornwel-Smith, who have been guides and companions in exploring this complex and colourful country. And grateful for the Thai friends I've made over the years.

Yet, after all this time, the difficulty of penetrating Thai society gives me continually the sensation that I'm seeing the whole thing go by as I speed behind a glass car window. Although a long-term resident, I'm still just a tourist here.

I have a secret career. It began when I was working for Oomoto, a Shinto foundation outside of Kyoto. In the 1980s, when Japan's religions started getting involved in interfaith confer-ences, Oomoto lent me to them as their translator and arranger. Thus I became a translator for Japan's Bud-dhist and Shinto religions.

When I left Oomoto and moved my base to Bangkok in 1997, I assumed that my religious translation days were over. But one day in the summer of 1999, I received a phone call from a woman in New York whom I'd known from Oomoto days. 'The United Nations is planning a worldwide gathering of religious leaders in New York next year,' she told me. 'It's to be called the Millennium World Peace Summit of Religious and Spiritual Leaders. This will be the biggest gathering of religions ever: cardinals from the Vatican, Protestant and Greek Orthodox bishops, sheiks and muftis from the Islamic world, Hindu holy men and Native American chiefs. Also leading scientists, like Jane Goodall, famed for her study of chimpanzees in Tanzania – they're all attending. Can you find some Thai Buddhist leaders to join the summit?'

Impressed at the idea that I might be able to go to New York and maybe meet Jane Goodall, I agreed. The problem was, I didn't know any Buddhist leaders. I asked around, and a Thai friend introduced Phra Rajavaramuni, rector of Thailand's largest Buddhist university, Mahachulalongkorn Rajvidhayalaya University (MCU). He was a leading Buddhist intellectual, having written a thesis comparing Buddhist teachings with the existentialist philosophy of Jean-Paul Sartre.

Thai Monks in New York

Saa and I travelled across town to Wat Mahathat, a large temple complex housing the university, just west of Sanam Luang parade grounds by the Grand Palace. I expected that we would sit on the floor in attitudes of respect, as one usually does with Buddhist monks in

Thailand. But instead, we were shown into an office where we sat on chairs facing Phra Rajavaramuni at a desk piled with papers. He quickly grasped the importance of the Millennium Summit. 'I'll take care of it,' he said, and called in his assistant Phra Maha Sawai, who appeared with a computer and took down our email addresses.

A few weeks later, we were summoned back to MCU, this time to watch Phra Maha Sawai deliver a Power-Point presentation to a room of orange-robed monks who headed powerful monasteries across the country. Among them there was a figure in white, Mae Chee Sansanee Sthirasuta, Thailand's most charismatic Buddhist nun, famed for bringing teenagers to meditate at her centre. Mae Chee Sansanee has her own website. What with Phra Maha Sawai's PowerPoint and Mae Chee Sansanee's website, it was dawning on me that Thai Buddhism has been quick to embrace modern technology.

New York wanted Thailand's Supreme Patriarch to attend the conference, but this was out of the question, due to the Patriarch's precarious health. After months of discussion, they finally chose the venerable 93-year-old Councillor Somdej Phra Putthakhosachan, number three in the hierarchy, to head the delegation. Sixteen other abbots from temples across the country would attend him.

Thai Buddhism, bound up with royal prestige, must be one of the world's best-organized religious bureaucracies. King Rama IV, who spent twenty-seven years as a monk before acceding to the throne, reformed the clergy, leaving behind the strictly controlled system we see today. This is starting to change as people who feel unsatisfied with mainstream Buddhism turn to new alternatives, such as *phra thu dong*, 'forest monks', who keep their distance from the Buddhist hierarchy while practising meditation at hermitages far from the cities.

Large new sects have established themselves in recent years, notably Dhammakaya, with its huge modern temple in Pathum Thani Province north of Bangkok. Nevertheless, unlike China or Japan, where Buddhism long ago fragmented into dozens of sub-sects, Thai Buddhism is still largely a unity.

Historically, Buddhism posed a problem for royal courts. In eighth- and ninth-century China, when tax-free monastic complexes began depleting the imperial treasury, the emperor ordered the temples burned and the monks defrocked. Buddhism revived after this, but never flourished as before. In Japan, the Imperial Court simply sidestepped the temples. The emperor moved his capital from Nara to Kyoto, leaving the temples of Nara to moulder away, far from the centre of power.

In Thailand, the King brought Buddhism inside the court. In the heart of the old royal palace of Ayutthaya stood the royal temple, which is duplicated today in Wat Phra Kaew, the Temple of the Emerald Buddha, inside the Grand Palace. Bound in close embrace with the King and his court, Buddhism did not fragment into conflicting sects. One could say that it's the great stabilizing force, the quiet centre around which the chaos of Bangkok revolves.

Enter one of Bangkok's temples, whether a grand royal one such as Wat Suthat or a small neighbourhood *wat*, and the calm of the Buddha envelops you. The uncertainties of life, noise and dust, even the *sanuk*, fade away in a transcendental moment. Wat Phra Kaew, even on its busiest days crowded with tourists, seems somehow to partake of this sacral quiet.

I knew that interfaith meetings are anything but quiet. Amidst the babble of competing dogmas, the monks would need to communicate, and translating for them would be well beyond my Thai language skills. So I called upon Num (my landlord) to help. And so in August 2000, Saa, Num and I flew to New York with the Councillor, Phra Rajavaramuni, and the rest of the Thai delegation. We gathered in the lobby of Don Muang Airport and knelt before the Councillor, who blessed us all.

In New York, for the opening of the summit, the monks (and nun) held a ceremony of blessing on the stage of the United Nations Assembly Hall. It was possibly the most prominent appearance of Thai monks on the world stage ever. They brought with them a bottle of holy waters from nine temples, which they were going to sprinkle into the audience, using bundles of fibres made from long-stemmed *yaa kaa* grass.

Ten minutes before the ritual began, we realized that the bundles of *yaa kaa* had been left in the hotel. Phra Rajavaramuni reacted with Buddhist unflappability.

'Any leaves will do,' he said. Num rushed outside and searched until he found a tree in the UN's Japanese garden and snapped off a branch. ('I apologized to the tree,' he explained. 'I said, "Sorry, but this is for World Peace." '). At the high podium they sprinkled the nine holy waters with leaves from the UN garden, and all went well. On the way down from the stage, Num noticed Jane Goodall seated in the front row. Suddenly she spoke to him. 'I collect religious objects,' she said. 'Could I please have those leaves?' So the Thais' sacred water sprinkler ended up in Tanzania.

Apart from such rituals, the point of the conference was networking, for rabbis to meet bishops, and muftis to shake hands with patriarchs. It was an experience rather like the 'Ecclesiastical Fashion Show' in Fellini's movie *Roma*. We spent our time immersed in the crowds that mark such interfaith events, colourful with lots of flowing robes, tall hats and jewellery.

The Garden of Religions

Back in the 1920s, Onisaburo, the founder of Oomoto, spoke of what he called 'the garden of religions'. The spiritual roots of all faiths are the same, he said, but depending on where the sprouts arise – in a hot or cold place, and with different historical and ethnic backgrounds – they take different shapes like a thousand multi-formed flowers. Onisaburo said it would be a bore if every flower in the garden looked alike, and that we should be thankful for the glorious variety of religions.

The delegation of Thai monks felt quite at home in the religious mixture at the UN because Thailand itself is a 'garden of religions'. This might not seem obvious in a country that is seen as a Buddhist nation (despite its roughly 4 per cent Muslim minority). But it was not always primarily Buddhist. The ancient Mons and later the Thais who settled here were animists; and the Khmer Empire that dominated Thailand for hundreds of years was for much of its history Hindu. Thailand retains all of these strains.

One could say that North Thailand, bordering the Mekong with its panoply of hill tribes, is more animist. The royal tradition of Central Thailand is more Hindu.

Four-headed Brahma, who grants all wishes, is everywhere in Bangkok. His most famous shrine stands at the Erawan Hotel corner, thronged by petitioners all day and night. When I made my first trip to Bangkok after the 'Voice on the Bullet Train' in 1989, one of the first places I visited was the Erawan Shrine. To this day it's a special place for me, even though the wish I made back then has not yet been granted. I don't give up hope, and I always try to remember to *wai* when I walk by the Brahma shrine outside my apartment building.

In addition to Brahma, you see Garuda (Vishnu's winged mount) in front of banks and government buildings, the trident of Indra, King of the Gods, on top of temples and palaces. Ganesha, the elephant-headed god,

Statue of four-headed Brahma, facing the four cardinal directions.

patron of the arts (and symbol of the Fine Arts Department), features in museums and theatres.

In Bangkok you also come across some very unusual Hindu gods, such as Trimurti, the five-faced combination of three deities: Brahma, Vishnu and Shiva. There's a popular Trimurti statue in front of Central World Plaza shopping centre which has got the reputation of being a god of love, and so is much patronized by teenage girls.

Neither Brahma nor Trimurti have many shrines in India. In fact, there's even an old tale that Brahma was cursed that he would not have shrines in India to be worshipped at. The Hindu cult in Bangkok has little to

Garuda: the royal insignia of Thailand.

do with Hinduism as we see it today in India; it has taken on a Thai character.

One of my favourite places in Bangkok is Devasthan (literally 'Place of the Gods'), the Brahmin Shrine, across the street from Wat Suthat and the Giant Swing. It's a small place, easily overlooked, but it lies at the heart of the royal Hindu cult which dates back to royal Ayutthaya. I did once manage to visit this temple at dawn for the 'Cutting of the Topknot Ceremony', which takes place annually in early January. While usually the Brahmins of Devasthan stay out of the public light, at King Rama X's investiture in 2019, the Brahmin priests took a starring role in the mystical ceremonies of enthronement.

As we enter the twenty-first century, the cult of Hindu gods flourishes more than ever in Bangkok. Many young

Mask of Ganesha, remover of obstacles and patron god of the arts.

people in the city are bored with mainstream Buddhism, so they turn to the Hindu gods. While Buddhism teaches us to face the facts and live with them, the Hindu gods provide hope of changing those facts. It's a bit like buying a lottery ticket.

Chinese gods have also made a home in Bangkok. Enter a Chinese shophouse, and it displays a little red shrine in the back somewhere with writing in Chinese characters, and a Chinese protective god inside. Even Thais with no Chinese background often keep Chinese divinities around them. At one point I was told by a fortune-teller that I needed to acquire the Three Gods of Good Fortune: Hok, Lok and Siu (Longevity, Wealth, Happiness). So I made a trip to Chinatown and purchased three ceramic statues of these bearded Daoist patriarchs. Perched high above my bedroom, just by the air conditioner, Hok, Lok and Siu look after me to this day.

Chinese temples abound, especially in Chinatown, of course. Some are Buddhist, others Daoist, but all are distinguished by dense eye-stinging clouds of incense, and the sound of people shaking boxes of sticks to tell their fortunes. Of the Chinese deities, the Goddess of Compassion, Guanyin (called Guan-Im by the Thais) has an appeal that extends beyond the Chinese community. Her gaudily decorated temple at Chokchai 4 in Ladphrao is crowded every day with people petitioning for divine mercy.

Spirits

One type of shrine in Bangkok, for sheer numbers, sweeps away all the Hindu, Buddhist and Chinese divinities together. These are the 'spirit houses', *saanphraphum* (shrine to the earth) and *saanjaothii* (shrine to the spirit of a place), that stand beside homes and buildings.

A spirit house usually takes the form of a small temple standing on a raised pedestal. Inside are miniature figures of 'the grandfather and the grandmother', with dancers, symbolizing the local spirits of the place, who need to be appeased by the people living on their land. The smallest huts and the highest skyscrapers, all may have *saanphraphum* or *saanjaothii* shrines.

Saanphraphum shrines with garlands: (*left*) Khmer-style, with Mount Meru spire; (*right*) Thai-style temple roofs.

Not only do people propitiate the place spirits, but most Thais believe in *phii*, or ghosts. From the point of view of modern real estate, the fear of *phii* helps explain why Bangkokians have been so quick to tear down romantic wooden buildings and replace them with the new. It's because these houses are haunted, the abodes of vengeful *phii*.

Old Japan had a rich tradition of weird and wonderful ghosts, who are enjoying a fresh life in recent years in *anime* films and *manga* cartoons. But in this new existence, they appeal to the eye for their charm and wackiness, but no longer to the heart, as no one seriously believes in them any more. Not so in Bangkok, where *phii* are still alive and haunting every street. Ghosts dominate novels, TV and movies. They embody the dark undercurrent that inspires expat writers to pen 'noir' murder mysteries. Shrines propitiate them, shamans exorcize them and they appear incarnate in the form of dolls and effigies with their own cults.

In 2015, a craze for *tukataa luuk thep* ('child angel dolls') swept Thailand. The big-eyed dolls, looking like a child of one or two, seem to have grown from an older tradition of *gumanthong*, a magical effigy of a little boy, thought to have the power of an unborn foetus. Compared to this darker precursor, the long-eyelashed cute 'child angels' have a brighter, more cheerful feel, and it's believed that carrying one around brings good fortune. At the height of their popularity, in 2016, Thai Smile airline even offered special promotion seats for 'child angels', although there was also pushback from other passengers who were afraid to

Left: classic Nang Kwak, the 'beckoning lady'; *right*: plump Nang Kwak at a hamburger restaurant.

sit next to them. Meanwhile, it was reported that the abbot of a temple in the outskirts of Bangkok had turned down multiple requests for cremation ceremonies of 'child angels'. The *phii* are not only alive, it seems, but also dead.

In addition to dolls and spirit houses, animism expresses itself in the phallus-shaped amulets that you find on sale at Chatuchak Market, and it can also be seen in traditional tattoos which instil the spirits of tigers and *nak* serpents into their bearers.

The word 'animism' is not quite right, as it makes us think of merely tree and land spirits. There are also plenty of other deities you see in Bangkok that one might call 'gods of daily life'. Most popular is Nang Kwak, the 'beckoning lady', who, kneeling with outstretched hand curving downwards, beckons luck into shops across the city.

Khmer Magic

Animism is much about magic – fortune telling, curses and counter-curses. The most powerful magic, it is believed, comes from the Khmers. Khmer witch-doctors are much feared, and Khmer writing features in tattoos and other ritual inscriptions. Mon-Khmer are the substratum of modern Thailand, the indigenous people, whose chthonian wisdom precedes the arrival of the Thai. So the Khmer are believed to hold the keys to mystery.

I once witnessed up close Khmer magic at work in Bangkok. Kevin, a Canadian friend of mine, was dating a young woman named Bok from Buriram. Bok and Kevin had had an affair, but as it was leading nowhere, Bok decided to do something about this.

One night, as a group of friends were gathered drinking wine at my apartment, Bok pulled out a small brown bottle. This, she declared, contained a few precious drops of the legendary *namman phrai* oil used by sorcerers as a love potion. She had received it from her father, who had inherited it from Khmer wizards before him.

Namman phrai is made, according to old belief, from the melted-down chin fat of the violently dead. Touch one drop of this ointment and you will surely fall in love. 'Don't touch it!' everyone yelled. But Bok smiled and said, 'Nothing to worry about, can't you see? It's sealed tight.' Kevin picked up the little bottle out of curiosity. And then he noticed: the entire surface, even the lid and the bottom, were covered with a film of oil that was coating his fingers. Bok had tricked him!

Well, what did it matter? Another Thai superstition. And then, in short order, Kevin fell heavily in love with Bok – and, as J. K Rowling could have told us, love artificially induced by magical potions never has a happy ending. Within a year Bok and Kevin had parted in miserable circumstances, and I'm not sure that he ever entirely recovered. Since then I take Khmer magic seriously.

So do Thai politicians. The battle between the pro- and anti-Thaksin factions from 2006 to 2009 was accompanied by a parallel war of magic. In their skirmishes of voodoo the leaders of the two sides enlisted masters of the dark arts to help them, performing ceremonies to cast curses on the opposing camps.

I don't know where I have ever been that I felt so surrounded by spirits. Even Japan, where most people are both Shinto and Buddhist, has, after all, just two major religions. Here we have three: Buddhism, Hinduism and Animism.

To these you need to add two more: Christianity and Islam. Early royal courts relied heavily on Muslim traders, so much so that Ayutthaya had districts devoted to Macassars and Malays. Bangkok has well-established Muslim neighbourhoods, such as the one near Soi Rong-namkaeng, where I used to live, as well as the area around the Jim Thompson house.

As for Christianity, few Thais are Christian, far fewer than Muslim. But when Christmas comes, Central World Plaza raises a huge Christmas tree, dazzling with fairy lights. More fairy lights and Christmas trees decorate the pavement along Rajdamri Road, where thousands of people go to promenade and take photos. Shops overflow with little Santas, and malls reverberate with 'I'm dreaming of a white Christmas'.

Amidst this great 'party of the spirits' going on in Bangkok, mainstream Buddhism is a sobre affair. Thai Buddhism derives from Sri Lankan Buddhism, and the Sri Lankans are the most serious, the Calvinists of the Buddhist world. Thai temples, especially the more prestigious ones, strictly enforce the *vinaya* (monastic rules), and this created all sorts of situations for me and Num to sort out during the Millennium World Peace Summit in New York.

The rules decreed that monks could not sleep on thick mattresses, so they removed the sheets and blankets from their beds and slept on the floor of their hotel suite. Num spent hours standing at the airline reservations counter ensuring that the monks were seated only next to men, as they cannot sit next to a woman. The lady at the desk kept asking 'Why?' 'I don't know why!' answered Num, 'But they just can't!'

Monks don't even have names of their own, as we learned after returning to Bangkok. The names we had been using turned out to be nothing but titles, and as our monk friends have risen in the hierarchy, their titles keep changing with them.

Mai Pen Rai

On the street we notice the superstitious aspects of Buddhism, the freeing of birds and turtles at festivals, the pasting of gold leaf on to idols. But at a deeper level, Buddhism is about emptiness, and the Thais, who take their Buddhism seriously, have absorbed that. They've been taught since childhood that everything in the world is illusion, that desires are the root of all evil, that life is fated by karma. Even the best karma is not as good as no karma.

In the real world, I don't get the impression that these

teachings have succeeded in dampening desires very much. At least not judging by my Thai friends, who dream of saving up enough money to build a home in the country for their parents, or the big-haired ladies in the department stores who hanker after Gucci and Prada.

But it does give people a kind of strength to bear the difficulties of life. When I'm sad or depressed, Saa or another Thai friend will simply say, 'Well, it's your karma.' Not very encouraging, that. But at another level, seeing all one's loves and dreams as nothing but emptiness brings freedom; it's a psychological release.

It's all summed up in the Thai expression *mai pen rai*, one of the first words that a visitor to Thailand learns: 'never mind', 'it doesn't matter'. *Mai pen rai* encapsulates the Thais' light touch. When I first started coming to Bangkok, I used to contrast it with the equivalent expression in Japan: *shikata ga nai*, 'it can't be helped', 'nothing to be done about it'. The Japanese approach seemed fatalistic; the Thai more devil-may-care. Over time, I've come to feel, however, that the Thais and the Japanese are basically saying the same thing. The difference is that the Thais say it with a smile.

Before coming to live in Bangkok, I had studied Tibetan Buddhism and also Japanese Zen. Zen preaches *Mu* ('nothingness'), but the *Mu* of Zen felt to me like an aesthetic concept, an idea for designing gardens, but not especially relevant to daily life. In modern Japan, people rarely refer to Buddhist ideas in daily conversation.

In Bangkok, people speak and think about Buddhism

all the time. Maybe the Japanese have been speaking of Buddhism all along, but I just wasn't listening. Mu turned out to be relevant after all. It took moving to Bangkok, where the surface is so pleasurable, but at the same time full of surprise and disappointment. Bangkok may be suffused with Hindu gods, *phii*, and other divinities, but for me, at least, Buddhism trumps them all. It's where to go in the end to seek solace, the emptiness beyond the kaleidoscopic swirl of forms and desires in the city.

Detachment and emptiness come balanced with the sheer joy in existence that the Thais call *sanuk*. One can certainly have a lot of fun in Japan, famous for its whimsical fashions and 'floating world' nightlife. Nevertheless, 'fun' is hardly the keynote of Japanese life. 'Patience', 'persevere!' – expressions like this which you hear every day in Japan, drive people to work so hard and be so creative.

But the Thais look to see if a thing is *sanuk* before they decide if it's worth the effort. *Sanuk* is such a stereotype of Thailand that the most popular internet portal to things Thai is called sanook.com. One can imagine *sanuk* as the logical result of Buddhist nihilism. If life is short, and in the end nothing truly matters, then one might as well enjoy oneself.

In my Japanese art collection there's a fan with iron ribs covered with yellow paper. Noble families used such fans to train children in Noh dance; the fan was so unwieldy that the child developed excellent control. Upon coming of age, the dancer acquired a real bamboo fan, and the lightness and freedom of use made dancing the easiest thing in the world.

For me, the iron fan symbolized Japan. The hierarchy and indirectness that so bedevils foreigners arriving in Thailand exist in far more elaborate forms in Japan – a dimension of difficulty above the bland Thai smile. When I made my official move to Bangkok in 1997, it seemed to me that, after a lifetime in Japan, Thailand should come easy.

Yet those decades of experience in Japan proved to be nearly worthless. For Thailand is truly a thing unto its own, and the Thai smile conceals shades of nuance that can make the stiff Japanese bow appear almost primitive.

Nothing was what I had imagined it would be. The City Pillar turned out to be two pillars. I investigated many a real estate venture, but found that land comes in several shades, from 'registered deed' to 'squatters' rights', to 'don't know'.

I imagined that I would become an art collector – but what had seemed so innocent and even spiritually uplifting in Japan took on darker overtones down here. So although I did make a collection, I ended up giving it back to the state. I set out to establish a programme of traditional arts – and instead I found myself back in school again. I rented an old Thai house, but although I spent many a magical night there, I never did live in the house and left it after fifteen years. What I did do was to run a shop selling *benjarong*, far from my basic interests, which closed, having lost all the money that my investors had entrusted to me. In short, all was evanescent, everything slipped through my fingers.

It's not just a matter of uncertainty in my personal affairs. The political landscape of Thailand also lies on shifting ground. In Japan, just as you can be sure that the trains will run on time, it's a comfort to know that few great changes will take place in our lifetimes.

Not so in Thailand, where the society rests on a seismic fault zone. The struggles between the Red and Yellow Shirts exposed deep fissures, and as we enter the 2020s everyone knows that further upheavals are in store. You can't assume that the same people will be in power when you wake up in the morning. Nobody can guess where Bangkok is heading.

Once I thought I knew something about antiques, performing arts, Buddhism, and the role that we foreigners play in Asia. Now, things appear rather different. Part of the experience has been a hard one, of disillusionment, coming to grips with the emptiness under the charming surface of things.

In any case, one had best be in the place that teaches one patience and some detachment – plus, of course, plenty of *sanuk*. As for the rest, *mai pen rai*. I came to Bangkok seeking much, but found just one thing for sure: home.

Appendix: List of Kings

Kings of the Chakri Dynasty

Rama I King Buddha Yodfa Chulalok 1782–1809

Rama II King Buddha Loetla Nabhalai 1809–24

Rama III King Nangklao 1824–51

Rama IV King Mongkut (Chomklao) 1851–68

Rama V King Chulalongkorn (Chulachomklao) 1868–1910

Rama VI King Vajiravudh (Mongkutklao) 1910–25

Rama VII King Prajadhipok (Pokklao) 1925–35

Rama VIII King Ananda Mahidol 1935–46

Rama IX King Bhumibol Adulyadej 1946–2016

Rama X King Vajiralongkorn 2016–present

Royal barge in front of the Grand Palace.

Acknowledgements

D ozens of people helped over the years with the writing of *Another Bangkok*. Firstly there was M. R. Narisa Chakrabongse of River Books, who published the original version in Bangkok under the title *Bangkok Found* in 2009. Professor Vithi Phanichphant was a fount of wisdom and wit concerning traditional Thai culture. Anucha 'Tom' Thirakanont, Peeramon Chomdhavat and Surat 'Kai' Jongda guided me to an understanding of Khon masked drama. Zulkifli Bin Mohamad introduced me to contemporary Asian dance. Dr Navamintr 'Taw' Vitayakul instructed me in Thai food, design and history. Writer Philip Cornwel-Smith gave advice during the book's long gestation.

I owe much to the readers of the book's many revisions: Vasit Kasemsap, Timo Ojanen, Paul Cato, Cameron McMillan, Ari Huhtala, Kristian Tuomikumpu, David Fedman, Moana Tregaskis, Toshiaki Yamada, Garrett Kam and Kathy Arlyn Sokol.

Thanks to flower artist Sakul Intakul for granting permission to use one of Jirasak Thongyuak's photos from Sakul's book on modern Thai flowers *Dok Mai Thai*; to Lanna artist Neti 'Bee' Phikroh, who drew the image of the *hatsidiling* (elephant-bird); Khanchai 'Jom' Homjan,

Khon mask maker and Instructor of Rajabhat Chadrakasem University, who drew the samples showing the development of *prajam yam* and *kranok* patterns of *Lai Thai* design; contemporary dancer Pichet Klunchun for allowing me to use a photo of him performing with elephant mask; Lanna dancer (and my partner) Ronnarong 'Ong' Khampa, who provided a photo of himself performing modern dance with *fon leb* fingernail extensions; and the National Archives of Thailand for permission to use historical photos.

Thanks to Ping Amranand, who supplied essential information about the Svasti family, and to M. R. Chakrarot Chitrabongse, who made sure that I didn't forget to mention the Traiphum cosmology.

I offer heartfelt appreciation to my staff, who stayed up late many nights, working on the photographs, illustrations, layout, indexing, research and fact-checking for the book: Tanachanan 'Saa' Petchsombat, Vitsanu 'Soe' Riewseng and Rachen 'Num' Suvichadasakhun.

ALLEN LANE
an imprint of
PENGUIN BOOKS

Also Published

Hanif Abdurraqib, *A Little Devil in America: In Priase of Black Performance*

Carlo Rovelli, *Helgoland*

Herman Pontzer, *Burn: The Misunderstood Science of Metabolism*

Jordan B. Peterson, *Beyond Order: 12 More Rules for Life*

Bill Gates, *How to Avoid a Climate Disaster: The Solutions We Have and the Breakthroughs We Need*

Kehinde Andrews, *The New Age of Empire: How Racism and Colonialism Still Rule the World*

Veronica O'Keane, *The Rag and Bone Shop: How We Make Memories and Memories Make Us*

Robert Tombs, *This Sovereign Isle: Britain In and Out of Europe*

Mariana Mazzucato, *Mission Economy: A Moonshot Guide to Changing Capitalism*

Frank Wilczek, *Fundamentals: Ten Keys to Reality*

Milo Beckman, *Math Without Numbers*

John Sellars, *The Fourfold Remedy: Epicurus and the Art of Happiness*

T. G. Otte, *Statesman of Europe: A Life of Sir Edward Grey*

Alex Kerr, *Finding the Heart Sutra: Guided by a Magician, an Art Collector and Buddhist Sages from Tibet to Japan*

Edwin Gale, *The Species That Changed Itself: How Prosperity Reshaped Humanity*

Simon Baron-Cohen, *The Pattern Seekers: A New Theory of Human Invention*

Christopher Harding, *The Japanese: A History of Twenty Lives*

Carlo Rovelli, *There Are Places in the World Where Rules Are Less Important Than Kindness*

Ritchie Robertson, *The Enlightenment: The Pursuit of Happiness 1680-1790*

Ivan Krastev, *Is It Tomorrow Yet?: Paradoxes of the Pandemic*

Tim Harper, *Underground Asia: Global Revolutionaries and the Assault on Empire*

John Gray, *Feline Philosophy: Cats and the Meaning of Life*

Priya Satia, *Time's Monster: History, Conscience and Britain's Empire*

Fareed Zakaria, *Ten Lessons for a Post-Pandemic World*

David Sumpter, *The Ten Equations that Rule the World: And How You Can Use Them Too*

Richard J. Evans, *The Hitler Conspiracies: The Third Reich and the Paranoid Imagination*

Fernando Cervantes, *Conquistadores*

John Darwin, *Unlocking the World: Port Cities and Globalization in the Age of Steam, 1830-1930*